What people are saying about

Emotional Repatterning

Clear and concise, Dr. Samet has offered a book that can create real emotional change for seekers once and for all. Dr. Samet's approach to full wellness starts with the emotional terrain we all find ourselves in — patterns of old thinking that do not serve us currently and that also threaten to interfere with living our best and brightest lives. *Emotional Repatterning* is courageous as it tackles the obstacles to being fully alive and present in our lives. It provides a step-by-step approach to anyone who is looking to heal at a deeper level, beyond where supplements, eating well and exercising can touch. By providing tools to change deep and long-held subconscious beliefs, Dr. Samet guides us in digging out from our past hurts, resentments, triggers and pain and reach higher ground. This book provides a valuable solution that every person could benefit from — change your beliefs and your biology will follow. An easy and enticing read that I could not put down.

Dr. Mary Shackelton, MPH, ND

I encourage you to buy this boo' and provocative dialogue of healing . Starting with the introduction's opening p. ok captivates while it teaches and informs. Given usive world of self-help books, I am always looking for one that stands out from all the rest. This book accomplishes that. Dr. Samet uses actual stories from her extensive professional career to illustrate timeless principles of personal and spiritual transformation. She begins her discussion of these principles by first sharing a deeply personal and poignant story from her own life; one that forced her and her family into crisis and transformation. The goal of her

sharing is to guide us, the reader, through our own life stories while reflecting on numerous wise and fundamental guideposts. The book helps us to identify and then shift our outdated and deeply held beliefs that keep us stuck. These outdated beliefs about ourselves and our lives often stop us from living full, authentic and joyful lives. Our dysfunctional thoughts and belief patterns aren't always obvious; and that's the problem! This book weaves together human stories, wisdom and life lessons in a way that has you looking at your own life from shifting perspectives - if you are willing to be honest with yourself. It is said that "The Truth Shall Set You Free." I found this book to be freeing for the many truths it unabashedly reveals. Give yourself this gift and take it to heart. You won't be disappointed.
Molly Punzo, MD

I found *Emotional Repatterning* to be life-changing. Dr. Samet draws on her decades of treating thousands of patients, her great curiosity about human existence, and her years of training in the realm of emotional healing to produce a book that can help virtually anyone suffering with anxiety, depression, anger and other forms of emotional distress. It is a book that has given me extraordinary insights into my own life – and a path forward that is free from despair and far more joyful and fulfilling than the path I long traveled.
Peter Gold, Senior Partner, Gold & Partners

Emotional Repatterning

Healing Emotional Pain by Rewiring the Brain

Emotional Repatterning

Healing Emotional Pain by Rewiring the Brain

Lisa Samet, N.D.

BOOKS

Winchester, UK
Washington, USA

JOHN HUNT PUBLISHING

First published by O-Books, 2021
O-Books is an imprint of John Hunt Publishing Ltd., 3 East St., Alresford,
Hampshire SO24 9EE, UK
office@jhpbooks.com
www.johnhuntpublishing.com
www.o-books.com

For distributor details and how to order please visit the 'Ordering' section on our website.

Text copyright: Lisa Samet 2020

ISBN: 978 1 78904 591 8
978 1 78904 592 5 (ebook)
Library of Congress Control Number: 2020933104

A CIP catalogue record for this book is available from the British Library.

Design: Stuart Davies

UK: Printed and bound by CPI Group (UK) Ltd, Croydon, CR0 4YY
Printed in North America by CPI GPS partners

The names of the people referenced in this text have been changed to protect their identity.

We operate a distinctive and ethical publishing philosophy in
all areas of our business, from our global network of authors to
production and worldwide distribution.

Contents

To three of the greatest teachers I could ever have:
Zoe, Zach and Ben

Acknowledgements

I would like to express deep gratitude to my early readers who provided invaluable feedback and encouragement on initial drafts: Jessica Samet, Sabine Karsenti, Donna Duseigne, Bianca Bayer, Coleen MacKinnon, Peter Gold, Scott Samet, Sitara Young, Mirella de Blasio, Mimi Bercovitch, Mimi Saine and Lise Higham. Even greater than this is my appreciation for your friendship and your love.

Thank you to Sabina Walser, Louise Harvie and Mary Shackelton for your deep friendship over the years and your encouragement as I discussed my early thoughts and plans for this book. And to Randi Samet and Arden Schneider, blood sister and chosen sister, who have been there since practically the beginning!

Enormous thanks go to my patients, from whom I have learned so much about what it means to show up every day with an open-hearted presence. Your trust and confidence in me has helped me grow as a person and as a doctor.

Thank you as well to my editor Melissa Kirk, Words to Honey, for your skill in restructuring, problem solving, improving, and encouraging me to keep honing my thoughts and words.

Finally, thank you to my family – André, Zoe, Zach and Ben – for believing in me and supporting me in this endeavor... and for your company on this great journey.

Introduction

Our lives are filled with great beauty. And great suffering, too. How can we make our journey easier?

The goal of this book is to deepen our understanding of the mind – the patterns of thinking and deep-seated beliefs that keep us feeling stuck and unhappy – so that we can learn what it takes to change: change both our thinking at the conscious level and our beliefs at the subconscious level.

Two Trains on Two Tracks

These two aspects of our mind are like two trains that run along different tracks. When we attempt to intellectually understand ourselves and sort out our problems, when we go to therapy to try to feel better, when we set resolutions and goals and say affirmations, we are using one part of our brain – our conscious, reasoning mind. But as you may have noticed, when we resolve to change things about ourselves with solely this conscious intention, it often doesn't happen.

That's because, resting underneath this conscious thinking is our more out-of-reach, and very powerful, subconscious mind. This is where our attitudes, values, experiences, long-term memory, habits and beliefs reside. So, if we don't align both aspects of our mind – the conscious and the subconscious – around our desire to change, we often end up with no change at all... simply frustration.

Amazingly, only about 5% of our brain activity is within our conscious awareness, the other 95% is subconscious – that's why it's so influential! If we ignore this part, our capacity to change our views and behaviors is very limited indeed.

What a shame, then, that the subconscious is often a minefield of limiting beliefs and old, outdated, negative "programs" that are not indicative of who we are, or who we want to become.

And it's fair to say, these subconscious beliefs we carry about ourselves influence all aspects of our lives, including our relationships, self-esteem, financial prosperity, career choices, even our health and weight.

Sadly, many of the beliefs we carry are not even accurate – they are often the result of a comment made long ago by a parent, teacher or even a kid in the schoolyard that caught us at a vulnerable moment – but we still believe them to be true, deep down. These beliefs may have also formed from conclusions we made about ourselves when we were young, often a result of the limited perspective we had as a child in a complicated adult world. This unexamined childhood programming, then, becomes our adult habits of perception and behavior.

Two-Pronged Approach

In order to move forward to create lives we are excited about living, we need a two-pronged approach for diminishing our emotional pain: addressing both the rational, conscious mind *and* the underlying subconscious tapes that often run the show. This is accomplished by straightening out "warped thinking" we may have at the conscious level, while also identifying and changing the underlying beliefs on the subconscious level that present the real obstacles to us moving forward.

My personal experiences and those of my patients has convinced me that working with our subconscious beliefs opens the way for changes we were previously unable to implement – and deeply solidifies them. It's the piece that's been missing until now, the golden nugget.

Working with thousands of patients over more than 20 years in my naturopathic practice, I've observed that our collective tendency to fall into certain "thinking traps" contributes greatly to our misery. But, despite working hard with patients to help them understand these traps and free themselves from the thought patterns that kept them stuck,

2

miserable and anxious – our efforts were often not enough for real and lasting change.

Out of necessity, I searched for other solutions – and found a body of work developed over the last few years on the power of subconscious beliefs. Deeply curious about this, and feeling that I was on the verge of understanding something very important, I educated myself in methods to work with my patients directly at this level. I learned techniques that helped them address the issues in their lives more effectively by identifying and changing their underlying limiting beliefs.

And these methods work! I began to see real and lasting change with patients on an emotional level, change that had, until now, eluded them. Patients who previously struggled, were now finding peace after rewriting old stories about their painful pasts in a more authentic way, with more ownership and a new perspective.

Many times people are motivated to look at their problems with a fresh perspective simply because they are tired of suffering. If you're reading this book, I'm guessing you may be there as well: finally ready to let go of the beliefs that hold you back from being fully present in your life.

Neuroplasticity

In order to explain how we can make these shifts in perspective, I'll start by illustrating the concept of neuroplasticity. Neuroscientists have recently discovered that the brain is actually affected physiologically by our experiences and interpretation of events. We now know that if we change the way we view our experiences, we can actually physically change our brain.

Simply stated, neuroplasticity is the ability of the neural networks in our brain to change based on information gathered through our experiences. The more often we have a thought, for example, the stronger certain neural networks in the brain become and the opposite is true of thoughts we have less often:

neural connections get weaker. What fires together, wires together!

Neuroplasticity research has given us a greater understanding of the capacity of our neurons to continue to grow and change, to reinforce new beliefs with repetition of new responses to old situations. This creates new patterns, which rewires and then hardwires the brain, allowing us to become unstuck, and move forward.

For example, if you were frequently criticized by a parent when you were a kid (when your brain was very malleable and forming its deepest neural networks), you may have developed an oversensitivity to criticism because the emotion of shame was triggered more often than, for example, the happiness of being praised. As an adult, you may have issues with low self-esteem and being hypercritical of yourself and others, which can lead to anxiety, depression, troubled relationships and other problems.

The good news is that by working on these internal messages, you can replace those old, negative thought patterns that got wired into your brain when you were younger – with more appropriate, supportive, and helpful patterns now as an adult. Your brain connections actually change in response to receiving this new input!

Neuroplasticity, then, has taught us that it is not our genetics but our beliefs that control our lives. Recent research on the brain has determined that the way we process life – how we perceive situations and events – is one-third inherited and *two-thirds learned*. Beliefs are simply conclusions derived from information and experiences, but they end up becoming filters for our reality. These filters are very powerful, but since our beliefs about the world and ourselves are learned, they can also be changed: we *can* learn a new way to perceive things!

Changing Our Thinking at the Conscious Level

It is essential to understand that a big culprit in our suffering is *our view* of the people and situations which seem to be causing us misery. Given that we can only change ourselves, and never other people (at least I've not had much luck with changing anyone else!), we can become empowered through understanding this basic fact. After all, if we are both the problem *and* the solution, then we have the power to change and move forward!

We Weren't Taught Emotional Wisdom

When I watched my kids go through school, I lamented that they were learning so many useless facts (forced to memorize various explorers in history who, for example, discovered particular lakes and rivers on certain dates, and farted on certain other dates) instead of skills that would equip them to cope with the challenges they would inevitably face in their lives. Why are we not taught from childhood how to better handle life's difficulties? Who among us is immune to them?

Wouldn't we all have been better served had we been taught more relevant material: How to resolve conflicts with one another? How to express difficult emotions, like anger, constructively? How to wade through the swamplands of grief and disappointment and emerge emotionally healthy on the other side of it? How to keep showing up for life in the face of injustice and disappointment without bitterness and cynicism? How to view our futures with optimism and hope, despite our past failures... and the state of the world? How to love and value ourselves through all of life's hardships, instead of blaming ourselves and others, feeling guilty or regretful? Now *that* would be a curriculum! Sadly, it wasn't offered to me, my kids, or anyone else I know.

Learning how to be present and skillful in the face of difficulty is not irrelevant, an option, an extra. It is essential. That we are seldom formally taught these things leaves us ill-equipped to manage our lives when difficulty strikes in our own backyard, as it did in mine. The vast majority of us have never been taught the skills that would enable us to manage our lives effectively when it gets difficult. Because who *could* teach us this? Our parents and teachers, who themselves had no idea? No one taught them!

The Eight Thinking Traps

This book covers eight main spheres where we commonly struggle with specific "thinking traps." These repetitive and negative ways of thinking not only make us suffer, they can also make us sick.

In Chapters 2–9, I delve into each of the eight areas, illustrating with examples from my life and practice how our emotions and thoughts can get tangled up in common patterns. Read carefully and see how often you recognize yourself in the case examples I present. Coming to a conscious understanding of the ways in which our interpretations of life create misery shows us exactly in which areas our thinking needs to evolve.

At the end of each chapter, I challenge you to look deeply at yourself for personal examples of these warped thought patterns to see if you are able to identify areas where you would benefit from re-writing old scripts. This is the first step in Emotional Repatterning.

Changing Our Beliefs at the Subconscious Level

Often, if we become miserable enough, we seek out a therapist. It can be so cathartic to air out our problems to a sympathetic listener who has the skills to guide us over rough terrain. But in my experience and that of many of my patients, conventional therapy stops there: we may have a greater understanding of our problems, but we are often still stuck to bring about real change in ourselves. So, we need to do better, go deeper, by moving beyond our conscious understanding of our problems and looking for the subconscious beliefs that underlie our difficulties.

Identifying limiting beliefs involves looking at the problems and obstacles which are challenging us, and digging deeper to find the roots of the distress. In Chapter 10, I will teach you how to identify your limiting beliefs as well as how to replace them with more accurate ones. I like to think of this as the ultimate "software update."

By addressing both our conscious and subconscious minds, we can make extraordinary shifts in our everyday lives – great enough to create a more hopeful and positive future for ourselves, opening up limitless possibilities and allowing us to experience more of life's beauty.

Chapter 1

Upheaval

Is this really happening to us?

When I got the call that our 10-year-old son Benjamin had fallen from a tall play structure at his sleepaway camp, I wasn't too concerned, even though the camp staff told me he had lost consciousness for a few moments. They reported that he seemed fine: no concussion, but when we talked to him on the phone, he cried that he wanted to come home. He had a big bruise on his leg and was shaken up from the fall. At the same time, Ben was really sad to leave camp and we agreed that if he felt better in the next few days we would drive him back to finish the two-week session.

Ben seemed more or less fine after he arrived home, aside from a few bruises and scratches. After resting up for a few days, he returned to camp for the remainder of the session. But even many weeks later, Ben seemed to have a multitude of aches and pains and was less energetic than usual. We brought him to see our family's osteopath numerous times over the remainder of that summer to be treated for his many small complaints.

Something Just Wasn't Right

In September, Ben started fifth grade. But as he was clearly not himself in some very indefinable way, I brought him to a lab to get a blood test, thinking he might be anemic. The results came back two days later, with a note from the overseeing doctor at the lab: "refer to pediatric oncology to rule out leukemia."

In fact, the red and white blood cell counts were only slightly out of the normal range, but what was concerning was the presence of lymphoblasts, immature white blood cells, which shouldn't have been present – and which indicated a potential blood disorder.

Maybe there was some mistake? I sent the results right away to my sister-in-law, a medical doctor, for a second look, and she forwarded them to her colleague, a pediatrician. My sister-in-law called me within the hour and told me the pediatrician said we should go straight to Emergency.

What? Still in denial, I asked if we could go the next day, as Ben had a swimming lesson that afternoon. "No!" was the emphatic answer.

André, my husband, was away on a business trip in Europe and I brought Ben to Emergency at the hospital that day, certain that there was another, better explanation for the results being a little off. The doctors took more blood, examined Ben and asked me many questions about his health over the previous month. Finally, after a very long afternoon, he was scheduled for a bone marrow biopsy the following morning to rule out leukemia.

André and I are both Naturopathic Doctors. At that point, we had been working together in our busy clinic for 16 years, treating patients with holistic therapies, homeopathy, lifestyle changes and nutritional counseling, all geared to encourage the body to heal itself. We have three children and have raised them with only the best: a diet of organic food and lots of fruits and veggies, enough sleep, outdoor activities and natural medicine when they were sick. We didn't even have cough syrup or Tylenol in our house!

We managed every cold, ear infection, gastro and injury quite well. Our children had excellent health – strep throats and flus would go through their classrooms and rarely did our kids catch them. Clearly, we were doing something right, but as importantly, we felt we were practicing what we preached, living in accordance with our values.

But now here we were, looking at the worst possible scenario – cancer. I could hardly breathe. How could this possibly be happening to *us*?

That night, I called André, telling him the news, looking for some reassurance that Ben couldn't possibly have cancer. He suggested maybe it was a virus, like mononucleosis, that could be causing the symptoms. When I had pleaded with the doctor earlier that day to offer me another possible diagnosis than leukemia, he also said it might be mono. The fact that they both came up with the same alternate explanation calmed me a little.

I'm not sure how I got through the night, alone in my bed, sobbing and shaking with fear, but we arrived back at the hospital the next morning at 8:30 a.m. for Ben's biopsy. I simply didn't have a good feeling about it, recalling Ben's lethargy over the previous few weeks, not to mention my maternal instincts that something *was not quite right* with Ben.

Not wanting to alarm my older two children, Zoe who was 15 and Zachary, 13, I got them off to school on time, simply mentioning that Ben was leaving late because he had a doctor's appointment.

The Diagnosis

The biopsy was completed uneventfully and we were told the results would be available at around 4 p.m. Ben played on his iPad all day, happy to be out of school. He was smart enough to sense something serious was happening, but didn't appear to be disturbed.

Finally, the doctor came into the room and announced to me, "We have the results back, why don't you come with me and we can discuss them in the conference room down the hall?" As I followed the doctor down the hall, a voice inside my head was screaming: "This must be bad news! If the results were good wouldn't she have just announced them to us in Ben's room?" I was numb and felt sick to my stomach. The walk to the conference room felt like a walk to Ben's death sentence.

Ben was diagnosed with leukemia, the most common cancer

in kids. I'll never forget the doctor or the room we were in, or the color of the round table we were sitting around. Time stood still. The shock and disbelief were overwhelming. I didn't cry; I was too stunned.

The good news was that the recommended treatment had about a 90% cure rate. The bad news was that it meant Ben would have to undergo two years of chemotherapy. Two years.

The Treatment

Despite everything – our beliefs, our philosophies, our values – we went ahead with the treatment. I can't say I have ever been a fan of modern medicine, which usually has a "treat the symptoms, not the cause" approach, but 90% is a very high number when looking at cancer survival rates. I could only hope that Ben's incredibly good health up until that point would help him tolerate the grueling two years that surely lay in front of him.

None of the doctors were ever able to tell me whether the fall at camp triggered his cancer, which in his case was the continuous repetition of damaged white blood cells with no shut off switch. They were able to tell me that it was not passed on genetically, but more like an "accident" in the reproduction mechanism of the cell. Call it a mother's instinct, but I'll always believe it had something to do with his fall. We'll never know.

Ben missed most of his fifth-grade year, mostly in the hospital, as he suffered almost every known side effect from the chemo, or at least it seemed that way to us. He lost all his hair, was too nauseous to eat most of the time and weighed as little as 47 pounds at one point, requiring a feeding tube through his nose and into his stomach. He got a blood clot from his catheter and was put on blood thinners. He even broke his arm after a simple fall because of severe osteoporosis from the leukemia and the prednisone, which was part of his chemo regimen. He got numerous infections and the doctors pumped him full of antibiotics each time, the same antibiotics that we had so successfully avoided earlier in his life.

But as intolerable as any one of these individual things were for me to witness, the worst was simply seeing my child suffer and being helpless to change any of it. Even worse: to be an accomplice to it.

There are many moments I desperately wish I could erase from memory, but the hardest are the ones of André and I carrying Ben into the car on treatment days with him crying, kicking, screaming and begging us, "Please, please I don't want to go, please don't make me go..."

I still have horrifying images that pass through my mind, often in the middle of the night: nurses in head-to-toe protective suiting administering bags of bright yellow or red chemo IV to Ben. Ben being wheeled away every few months to get a lumbar puncture with chemo to his brain, where leukemia cells like to hide and multiply. Ben spitting saliva into tissues for days on end after each weekly treatment because he was so nauseous he would simply salivate and spit, salivate and spit. We went through a minimum of two boxes of tissues within a few days after each treatment. I could go on and on.

The Results

Ben lived. He has been in remission now for over three years. Acute leukemia is so rapidly multiplying that if it was to come back, it would have by now. Ben graduated elementary school on time. He's now in tenth grade and in fabulous shape; to look at him, one would never know what he suffered – what our family suffered.

None of us are immune. The protective bubble that I unconsciously believed we had built around our family, affording us some protection because we had done "everything right" had, in fact, failed us. The medical establishment that I had built a career philosophically opposing had saved my son's life and I could only be eternally grateful.

A Gift of Insight

Through this incredible and prolonged suffering, I was broken open. My heart was cracked wide open. All I had counted on had failed me, failed Ben. And our family was forever changed in so many big and small ways. When a child gets sick, the experience alters all the family relationships and dynamics from that point forward. Sometimes bonds get stronger, but sometimes tensions develop that never fully heal.

Through my grief, I came to understand suffering in a different way. Sure, I had experienced pain before in my life – with relationship breakups and the death of my parents – but nothing compared to this.

From this new vantage point, however, I was left with a gift of insight. I was better able to understand the nature of life and suffering with a clarity that I still find hard to explain. I now have a certain intuitive knowledge when working with patients, of their emotional blockages and stuck areas. I see these blocks and feel them as if they are my own.

I remember during the darkest moments of Ben's treatment – when the possibility of his death from the treatment's side-effects loomed large – tapping into an eternal well of human suffering: how many mothers through time had seen their children become ill, or die? How many had seen untold suffering and had been forced to witness it helplessly, unable to change anything at all? How many people on the planet at this very moment were living in a constant state of misery, injustice, cruelty, fear or pain? I was in very good company indeed. This perspective helped me weather the storm.

I worked to accept that this was, in fact, happening to us and that I was not "entitled" to anything better than so many others through time had experienced. I chose to accept what was, not fight it. It felt like a more honest approach: it was happening;

therefore I would be fully present for it.

I knew that Ben's life and the outcome of his treatment had many stakeholders and that I could only do my piece. Ben needed to do his piece, too, which was to fight for his life and have the will to keep going. And I recognized that the Universe had the biggest say, and that prayer could only help. We are all co-creators of the future and can only manage our own part of the story. I vowed to do my part as well as I could.

As is often the case with deep suffering, the resulting personal learning was enormous. Believe me, I would never have consciously chosen it, but I owed it to myself to wring the most understanding out of that time as I could. Intuitively, I knew that if I learned whatever I could going through it, my suffering would diminish, even if only slightly, and I would gain wisdom.

The experience I lived with Ben fueled my personal growth and ability to understand human nature more deeply. And, happily, that infused my professional life with greater abilities to work with patients on an emotional level.

Homeopathy

Professionally, I had been working with patients over the years in a variety of capacities, mostly using homeopathy. I love homeopathy because it has the potential to stimulate healing on all levels: physically, mentally and emotionally.

After an extensive first interview with a patient, I select one remedy to treat the whole person. If a patient arrives with six complaints – say headaches, depression, eczema, hair loss, warts and constipation – I see this as essentially one imbalance, and looking at the whole, and select one homeopathic remedy for the patient, not six different remedies, one for each problem. This is one of the beautiful aspects of this system of medicine – we don't see a person as parts, but as a whole organism. Similarly, we don't treat the disease, but the person.

The patient's reaction to the remedy is a trigger, or a wake-up call, for the body to begin to rebalance and heal itself. Over time, as the patient regains their health, they need the remedy less and less often.

Homeopathy works in a completely different paradigm than conventional medicine. A well-chosen remedy triggers a healing mechanism in the body, meaning symptoms actually heal from within, not by relying on an outside substance which must be taken daily and often indefinitely, in order to feel better. Thus, homeopathy offers a very different approach compared with daily dosing of meds for symptom-management, which is so much of what conventional medicine offers today.

Over the years, however, I couldn't help but notice that as well as most of my patients were doing, some of them were not helped as much on the emotional level by a homeopathic remedy that was helping them in so many other areas. This nagged at me. If a remedy was helping their itching and their headaches and their heartburn and their PMS, why wasn't their emotional distress also being alleviated in equal measure, as it was with many other patients? As we are treating the whole person, we expect every aspect of a person to show at least some improvement from the remedy.

I wondered whether the explanation might have to do with the patient's *interpretations* of their lives that was causing them pain, rather than an actual chemical imbalance. I became certain that one of the big obstacles in healing emotionally was this tendency to view life with certain misperceptions, which then became ingrained habit, leading to anxiety and depression and feelings of being *stuck*.

We all know how easy it is to lapse into habitual ways of thinking and feeling, which can form a "default mode" in our brains. Thus, warped patterns of thinking over time, on constant replay, become our reality.

Suffering Is Often a Great Teacher

I've often observed that people seem to learn mostly as a result of their desire to stop suffering. When things are going well, we typically don't do much self-work or self-inquiry. We are eager to show up for the good times, the high points, which don't involve much soul searching. When difficulty strikes, whether it be divorce, the sickness of a child, ill health, grief or financial loss, the ensuing stress forces us to go deep inside to find ways to cope. We often do this with the help of a therapist, or at least good friends. It's a hard and lonely path without any help.

From this struggle, though, comes growth: a new way to hold the difficult experiences, a new way to move forward through them. As we emerge from the difficulty, we have grown; we have accumulated wisdom. This is what it means to evolve.

We become wise through struggle and the creation of a new way forward. And, it is through these struggles that many of us start to ask those age-old questions: Why am I here? What is the purpose of my (relatively) brief stay on this Earth?

The alternative to choosing this growth path is often anxiety and depression. When we conclude that life is too hard, that there is no purpose to life, that we have lost our way, or that we have poor skills with which to manage its challenges, we can feel defeated. Sometimes we feel we have no choice but to turn to anti-depressants or anti-anxiety pills simply to function in our jobs and families.

My Paradigm

Throughout many years of working with people, reviewing research, experimenting with non-ordinary states, reading psychic and channeled material, studying Buddhism and Hinduism, and my own deep suffering and self-inquiry – I've come to the following conclusion: we are here on Earth to learn, and then to return Home at the end of the long "school year" as more evolved souls. And if we imagine for one moment this to be true, we begin to see everything through a whole different lens.

Try this on:

Earth is a boarding school. We agree to come here for a period of time, leaving our home in the spiritual realm. There is a curriculum which we co-create before we arrive, similar to choosing our classes before the semester starts, according to our goals for learning. We select a body to enable us to have the best experience with which to achieve our mission. Our ultimate goal: for our consciousness to evolve. When the learning is complete for this lifetime, we return home from school.

How does it fit?

I believe this to be true, and it's through this lens that I see and evaluate my own life.

Ask yourself, is it *possible* that this paradigm might true? And if it *were* true, how might you approach your life differently?

Seeing our lives on Earth from this perspective, it suddenly all looks quite different. For example, we would know that as students here to learn, we need to be much more tolerant of our mistakes: after all, what second grader knows advanced math? Which high school student is equipped to write a PhD?

If we were perfect and already knew everything, we wouldn't be here in school in the first place. Clearly that we are here, we have things to learn. So why not have the courage and the presence to look and see where we are weak and what we need to focus on to improve, with a curious, eager attitude? Then we could advance more easily through the lessons we have come here to master, without resistance and defensiveness. Without as much fear. But change is difficult, isn't it? Is it really worth our effort?

Yes, it is! Because with some courage and curiosity, we *can* untangle our difficulties – by first making peace within ourselves. This is because our primary relationship *is* with ourselves. If there is no acceptance, love, gratitude, respect there... it is very difficult to be present in a meaningful way for others. This work is the work of repatterning the emotions.

The Mind-Body Connection

Emotional disturbances affect our physical health, there's no doubt about it. We have probably all experienced this in a minor way: coming down with a sore throat after a stressful week at work – and some of us in a major way: being diagnosed with cancer a few months after a divorce, for example. Undoubtedly, our mental/emotional state has an effect on our immune systems and our immune systems are what protect us from disease.

Study after study has revealed similar findings: people who rated their sense of well-being as "high" had an average life expectancy of ten years longer than those who rated it lower. Self-rated "happiness" levels were positively correlated with good health outcomes in recovery from such diseases as diabetes, AIDS, stroke, heart disease and hip fracture. In a Dutch study of elderly patients, death rates were 50% lower among those with a positive mental attitude. Across the board, lower mortality rates are well correlated with positive psychological states and high life satisfaction.

Martin Seligman, one of the founders of "positive" psychology, studied the differences in health among people who tested as optimists versus pessimists. And guess what? People with a positive outlook are 45% less likely to die from *any cause* compared to pessimists, and a whopping 77% are less likely to die from heart disease! Optimists also catch fewer colds than pessimists, have lower blood pressure, have stronger immune systems and generally live longer.

Further, depression affects more than 21 million Americans annually and is the leading cause of disability for those 15–44 years old. It is also the main cause of over *30,000 suicides* in the US each year. Currently, about 20% of the population takes psychiatric medications, mostly antidepressants.

These numbers are staggering.

When we feel chronic depression, anxiety, hopelessness, helplessness or pessimism, these emotions activate the stress response in the body. Though some temporary stress is normal, long-term stress levels can lead to weaker immune function resulting in higher levels of infection, inflammation and disease in general. In a word, happier and more optimistic people enjoy greater health and lower mortality.

Feeling Stuck

Despite this, many people feel stuck to change themselves: "I was born pessimistic… my father's like that, it's genetic, isn't it?" or, "After the abuse I suffered in my childhood, how can I be optimistic? Easy for you to say!"

It's important to realize we are not stuck! There are many tools and techniques that have emerged in the last few years to help us make deep changes within ourselves and become *un-stuck*. More than ever before, we can learn to leave the past behind us and write a new script for our future.

It's true for most of us that real change at a deep level can be difficult. Looking at ourselves and our lives with objectivity is hard work. We're often too wrapped up in our stories to see things clearly. Sometimes when we do have the courage to look honestly, we don't like what we see. Even when we are able to acknowledge our suffering, we often don't know what to do about it. See a therapist? Who wants to dredge all of *that* up? Many don't want to expose themselves to a stranger. Shame, pride and feeling overwhelmed, not knowing where to start unravelling the mess, can continue to keep us stuck.

Come with me now to explore the eight specific areas I've uncovered where our thinking easily gets distorted, resulting in thought patterns that make us suffer. Using our conscious, rational mind, let's better understand these pitfalls and see how we can work with them or better yet, avoid them altogether. This is the first step in Emotional Repatterning.

Chapter 2

Self-Love

It all starts here...

Liz, 62, came to see me with a diagnosis of lymphoma. She had tried chemo with initial success but then the tumors came back in full force. She now wanted to try an alternative approach, using lifestyle changes and homeopathy. A homeopathic interview is very thorough – up to three hours long – and I get to know a person very well in that time. During the course of our interview, it was apparent that Liz had had a rough childhood. Her mother had been very critical of her, to the point of abusiveness. Nothing Liz did ever seemed good enough. Sadly, as an adult, Liz had internalized that critic and was extremely hard on herself. She was extremely critical of everyone else too, if not out loud, then certainly in her head.

I Hate Myself

Sadly, Liz felt she could do nothing right, that she was not nice looking, and not a good person because she had negative thoughts about other people all the time. She was constantly critical of others in her mind, judging them as stupid, lazy and inferior.

I asked Liz why she was so tough on herself. Her answer was point blank that she was filled with self-hatred. And, while Liz hated herself for thinking this way, she couldn't help it.

What a toxic soup! It would be hard to imagine her immune system being strong enough to fight cancer in that environment of hatred. While I did prescribe homeopathy and lifestyle changes for Liz to strengthen her immune system to better fight the cancer, I deeply felt the most important treatment I could offer her was to help her resolve her self-loathing. There was no way to prove that the cancer was related to this unrelenting negativity, but I certainly suspected it was a major factor. These types of thoughts are so stressful to the immune system that, when we understand the mind-body connection, it would be hard to believe they were unrelated!

It's difficult at best to live with the effects of lack of self-love. It results in a distortion of our fundamental sense of well-being, and most of us don't understand that it is the cornerstone of many of our problems.

While we often have a natural tendency to look inside ourselves for the causes of our problems, I've found that it's not necessarily important to find out why or when or how self-love was lost. It may be related to our upbringing, usually well-meaning parents doing a poor job (after all, who educated *them* in any of this?), or teachers or the educational system that left us feeling stupid or alienated, which can lead to our subconscious conclusion that *we're* the problem. Often, though, it's not at all obvious why we have a lack of self-love, or even that it's at the root of much of our suffering.

Lack of self-love can show up in many different ways. It can be a relentless internal critic that constantly tells us how we don't measure up. This can extend beyond a lack of self-love, even to self-hatred, as it did in Liz's case. When we don't love ourselves, it can also manifest as a deep aching void inside that yearns to be filled. We may search for that love from the outside, anything to fill the emptiness. This can result in us over-extending ourselves, as in offering inappropriate generosity or kindness in an attempt to "buy" the love from others. Sadly, this doesn't work and often we feel resentful when we continuously give of ourselves and others still don't meet our needs.

Lack of self-love also shows up when we simply don't take care of ourselves. Not wanting to be "selfish," we put our own needs last. Remember that safety warning on airplanes about putting the oxygen mask on yourself before putting it on your child? Why do you think they say that? Because an unconscious parent is useless to their children or other loved ones. It's not an example of our goodness when we consistently put others before ourselves. How can we be there for others *unless* we are well ourselves? Ideally, we need to change the view that taking care of ourselves, or putting our own needs first at times, is selfish.

If I don't love myself, how can I really love you? If I can't be kind to myself, forgive myself when I make a mistake... how can I offer that to you? I can't. It's impossible. We can't give what we don't have. Liz was too impoverished emotionally to give anything to anyone. I knew that how she felt toward others would soften as she came to love and respect herself. We had to start there.

When we are hard on others, it's almost always the case that we are equally, if not more, hard on ourselves. It looks like this: if I set the bar really high for myself and am always struggling to be perfect, it's very hard for me not to be critical of you if you are not working as hard as I am. I'm so angry that I have to work so hard to be right, good and perfect all the time, that I see you as a total slacker if you have lower standards for yourself than I do for myself. Only when I lower the bar for myself and can breathe a bit, can I be less critical of you. So, being more accepting of others has to start with being more accepting of myself. In fact, loving myself.

We all have a story. My mom didn't do this and my dad did too much of that. True, some stories are worse than others, and involve shocking tales of abuse or outright neglect. Can we still love ourselves? Can we still see ourselves as valuable and worthy of love? From this place of self-love and self-acceptance, and a recognition of our value and worth, not for what we do, but just because we *are*, emerges a gentleness and kindness. From this softer place, it is easier to extend a more authentic gentleness and kindness to others. For Liz to reach this softer place would be essential to her recovery.

We worked hard over numerous sessions to reconnect Liz with herself. We changed limiting beliefs that Liz had about her value, worth and lovability. (More on how we worked on changing her subconscious beliefs in Chapter 10.) Through this process, Liz came to see herself as the good person she was deep inside. She began to believe that she was worth saving, and also that her body could heal itself in this new environment of love and with a renewed intention to live.

Miraculously, the emotional work we did in combination with remedies, dietary changes and supplements resulted in the tumors shrinking. Moreover, she is more at peace with herself and others than she ever remembers feeling.

Our Flame

The way I see it, we all have a small flame burning inside us. We are born with it. If we imagine an immense candle burning, the Universal flame if you will, we know that our individual candle is lit from that same flame – we are many smaller candles that contain this light, from the same original source, the same original flame. Thus, the flame that animates me is the same flame that animates you. We are all connected by that flame. Can I recognize that flicker, that flame inside me, with awe? Can I see that you and I are connected, united by this same light? When I love, recognize and value myself, then and only then, can I extend it to you and accept it from you. And with that, there is a softness that was not there before: a place for healing to occur.

The Problem with Perfectionism

I think the most common area where I see a profound lack of self-love is with people struggling with eating disorders. In the patients I have worked with, the degree of self-hatred present is very painful to witness.

Robin came to see me at age 20. She had been struggling with eating for a few years. The previous year had been particularly painful and she had to come home early from her freshman year at college because things were getting way out of control. She was having a harder and harder time managing the cycle of eating and vomiting.

Like many people with anorexia, Robin was a perfectionist. She had an extremely high standard for herself. She used food to reward herself for reaching her goals – whether it was how much time she spent at the gym on a given day, how few calories she was able to consume by a certain hour, or even how much studying she was able to get done in a particular timeframe. If she "failed" she was not allowed to eat. If she did well, she allowed herself some food, though if she lost control and overdid it, she would be forced to vomit as that itself would be a failure. In a word, she was tortured.

She easily described her self-perceived failings to me and how much she hated herself. In fact, she also felt that others frequently fell short and she was overly critical of them as well.

I explained my theory to Robin: it's impossible to be so critical of oneself and yet be kind and loving to others. Only once you relax the standards for yourself can you be more tolerant of others' "averageness." Robin agreed.

But could she loosen her impossibly high standards? She was not optimistic about being able to do that, they felt woven into her fabric. Robin's self-hatred could not possibly abate while she was failing left and right – and it was impossible not to fail before the standards she set for herself each day! We were able to determine that subconsciously Robin believed that if she was able to perform impeccably, she would finally be deserving of the love – from others and from herself – that until now had been eluding her.

But clearly this logic was a problem. The self-love must come first, not the "performance." If we only feel self-love based on the results of our performance, in any arena of life, it is conditional love. Genuine self-love is never conditional. It is there simply because we exist and recognize ourselves as innately deserving of love.

In Robin's case, we worked on changing her beliefs about herself, her lovability, her safety. We rewired her beliefs about food as nourishment for her body, not as a reward for her behavior. We re-connected her with struggling humanity, each of us being on our own path, trying our best, deserving of love and encouragement for our efforts, not criticism and constant berating. With more kindness toward herself came more kindness in her internal dialogue toward others, as well as an easing up of the tight control her eating disorder had on her. The last time we spoke, she was working and applying again to university to continue her education. "A work in progress," as she describes herself.

Struggling to Find Validation

When we don't love ourselves, we will do most anything to fill that emptiness. We will do what we need to do to "buy" the love from the outside, attempting to compensate for the inner love we lack. This results in "pleasing behaviors," believing that if we are good enough, nice enough, that others will love us. It's our attempt to substitute others' love for the love we don't feel for ourselves, a yearning for love and recognition from the outside. I've seen this often with people who are overly generous, always there for everyone else. Or, those that bend over backwards to get recognition from others. While obviously acknowledgement and appreciation feel good, they can never substitute for the love we would ideally have for ourselves.

Iris, at 34 years old, was exceptionally bright. She was born in the US, but grew up in Asia when her Dad was transferred there for his job as a diplomat. Her parents were busy and very involved in their ex-pat social life. Iris was an only child, and suffered from their busyness, feeling very alone and unseen through most of her childhood. What her parents did notice, though, were her good grades. When she got her report card with all As they would beam with pride. When she was called up on stage to receive academic awards at the end of the school year, her parents were in the front row. She worked very hard to get the lead role in the school play and her parents clapped the loudest on opening night. She quickly learned that the best way to capture their attention was to be the best. So, she worked harder and harder to excel so she was always assured of their love and attention.

At 34, Iris had her PhD and was teaching at a prestigious university. She was the youngest star her department had ever had. But she was having trouble getting her papers published, papers that would assure her tenure. The difficulty was more an issue of bad luck than anything else: with one paper, her co-author fell ill and took a leave of absence, so the paper was put on hold. With another, the data had not come in as they expected and it was difficult to support their arguments as planned, so they had to scramble to find a way to best incorporate the data. She had a third paper under review with a journal and was terrified of rejection as the window to apply for tenure was closing.

When Iris came to see me, all she could talk about was the importance of getting the tenure and checking off that box... about how stressed and nervous she was as the deadline to apply for it was growing nearer and her three papers had not yielded any publication as yet. When I asked her why it was so important for her to get tenure, she told me because it would be embarrassing if she didn't get it. That everyone in the department expected she would get it, as they thought so highly of her. Distilled to its roots, she was longing for the praise and recognition from her colleagues in order to find value. Similar to when she was a child under her parents' roof, she was looking to others for the praise and acknowledgment she needed so she could feel "loved." The past has a way of repeating itself...

When we learn to look to the outside for self-value, self-worth and self-love, it's a losing game. That's because it's impossible to manage outside forces very well. We simply cannot manage or control others' opinions of us and this unending need for acknowledgement – impossible to truly fulfill – often leads to frustration and burnout. The goal was clear – to transform Iris' need for external affirmation to a reliance on self-love and self-acknowledgement. But how to change years of conditioning?

Because Iris was so smart, she understood things quickly. We discussed what might happen if she didn't get published and therefore didn't get tenure. She had been so focused on chasing that goal, she had never allowed herself to really consider that. But as we explored that option, she realized that all the stress and pressure had taken much of the joy out of her professional life. She had sacrificed a lot of time with her two young daughters in order to stay professionally "on track." She was able to see that leaving the university setting, should it come to that, and bringing her work into the business world might actually be more personally rewarding. She had never allowed herself to think about other options before, so as to not lose her momentum.

Through our work, Iris learned that "she" and "the work" she produced were two separate things. That as long as she produced work she felt good about, that was most important – feeling she had done her best. A publication would be fantastic, but as she was not in control of that happening, she couldn't allow her self-worth to rest on that. In fact, we agreed, if a paper wasn't published, it was not necessarily a comment on the quality of her work. Journals select articles for publication based on many different criteria (interests of their readership, theme of the publication, biases of the editors, etc.) not just the excellence of the paper. By wrapping her self-esteem around whether a journal published her work (and therefore "approved "of her), she was setting herself up for disappointment.

After we cleaned up these warped areas in her conscious thinking, we proceeded to work on changing some of her underlying subconscious beliefs. We worked hard over a number of sessions, always digging deeper to try to get to the core beliefs that were causing her misery. The goal was to update her old beliefs to something closer to the following: "I love myself," "My opinion of myself matters most," "How I see and value myself is more important than how I am seen and valued by others," "My work and professional efforts are separate from my value as a person," "How my work is evaluated is separate from how I see and evaluate myself."

At the end of our work together, Iris had a very deep understanding that she was not the work she produced: that she herself was lovable and had value, regardless of how she performed, or how others evaluated it... and that all she could do was her best, and then let go of the outcome, knowing that she had many options to use her talents going forward.

Desperate to Please

Janine, 53, came to see me to help her lose weight. She had gained and lost the same 100 pounds over and over again in her adult life. When she was single and hoping to attract men, the weight would come off, but then she would regain it shortly thereafter once she was settled into a relationship.

She was hoping I could recommend an effective eating plan and, more importantly, help her keep the weight off once she lost it.

Janine filled me in on her life. She was the seventh of 10 children. She had a career as a graphic artist and was very talented. She was also much loved by her co-workers and was often told she was incredibly helpful. If the boss needed someone to stay late to meet a deadline, Janine was there. If a colleague needed a ride, Janine would go way out of her way to offer it. If anyone needed something done, they knew they could count on Janine. Janine was very proud of this, but I was hearing something quite different.

I asked Janine when her weight problems began. She remembered herself as a young child, happy and carefree. At a certain point, maybe around 8–10 years old, she remembers thinking that her older sisters were so gorgeous and accomplished (in fact, one of them grew up to be a model), that she didn't have a chance of measuring up to them. She felt that the only way to be noticed and loved in her family was to be the most helpful and generous of everyone. So, no matter what her parents needed, she did it. Her father loved good food and she became an excellent cook so as to make his favorite dishes. As she got older, it didn't stop there. Any sibling in need, even to this day, could call on Janine for money or extended babysitting if they were stuck.

Why was Janine so desperate to please everyone? Was she trying to buy love with favors? Why the need to "buy" love? I suspected that Janine didn't love herself. Could that belief have snuck in there around age eight, when she concluded that all her siblings "had more to offer" than she had? Possibly. When I suggested that to her, Janine disagreed – she could name all her professional accomplishments easily enough, had raised two fine boys and was happily married. In her conscious, reasoning mind she did love herself – look at all her accomplishments! But deep down, in the place that matters most – her subconscious mind – it was clear to me that she did not.

In trying to fill the void that her lack of self-love had created, Janine was exhausting herself by the extremes that she went to to garner the admiration and love of others. But as discussed earlier, the love of others, no matter how gratifying, cannot replace self-love. And because, despite all her efforts, she still felt empty inside, she ate. She ate in an attempt to fill the void in another way. She also ate because of how exhausted she was, fulfilling the demands of others who had come to depend on her as their "go-to" person. She felt she couldn't escape this role, she had trained everyone around her very well to ask for anything and expect her to fulfill their demands!

As we talked more about it, Janine came to see that it was true – that her behaviors were calling out for love because underneath, she did not feel lovable. She could offer me no good reason why she didn't love herself. She told me what a good person she was inside. And, ironically, many of the siblings whom she had admired so much when she was young had grown up to be not very nice or accomplished people themselves.

Janine was ready for change, and importantly, she had never approached her weight problems from this point of view before. She could recognize that if she were to truly love herself, and therefore be able to put her own needs before others, she would have no trouble saying no to people. We worked on replacing her old beliefs with better ones: I love myself, I have infinite worth and value, I am safe, I set boundaries with ease, I know my needs and take care of them, I eat to nourish myself, to name a few.

The hope was that once Janine was living a life more aligned with her truth, her needs and desires, her internal stress would be greatly diminished and the need to overeat to comfort herself would be manageable.

She agreed to an eating plan that was not a diet, a plan where she would gradually lose weight and be able to maintain it.

Janine felt a lightness that she recognized in herself from almost 50 years earlier, when she was a child. She felt she had recalibrated herself, and was eager to move forward in the world loving herself, rather than seeking love from the outside. Her eating habits shifted radically, as she was able to check in with herself and notice when she was really hunger versus starving for love, and when she became full so she could end the meal.

Challenge

Close your eyes and go deep inside. Can you feel your love for yourself? Can you feel your soft heart, your efforts to do well, the innocence of your struggle? It begins here.

Take a few moments each day to check in with that love. Feel it when you are tempted to criticize and berate yourself for how you should have done better. Feel it when you have the reflex to put your own needs last and consider everyone else first. Remind yourself that this is not selfish, but mandatory: to care for yourself and attend to your needs. No one will do this for you, and it's no one's place to do it but yours. Only from fullness within can we give freely and generously, without a hidden agenda (one that may even be hidden from ourselves!).

Chapter 3

Acceptance

The gap between how things are and how we think they should be is equal to the degree of our suffering...

In working with patients, and in coming to a better understanding of the challenges in my own life, I came to understand that *accepting* what is in front of us, whether it is a situation or someone's behavior, can often be extremely challenging to do. However, a lack of acceptance is the source of incredible suffering for many of us.

The Expectation Gap

Why would the way another person behaves be a source of suffering for me? It's because we can easily interpret the way a person behaves as having, in some way, to do with *us*... as having some bearing on who *we* are... reflecting on us as somehow not good enough, or at fault. Instead of seeing the situation or the other's behavior as a result of who *they* are, we see it as a comment about who *we* are. When we are unable to change the dynamic or the behavior of the other (because, of course, we can never change anyone else, only ourselves), we suffer.

Many people have problems with this word acceptance. "No," they cry, "This is unacceptable! How can I accept *this*?" I would say, "How can you *not*?" It is simply the way it is. We must strive to accept situations and people the way they are. To do otherwise is a recipe for our own suffering (not theirs). When we align our expectations of situations and people in accordance with the situation *as it actually is*, we suffer less, as there is no gap between what we expect and the reality.

One way to make this easier is to realize that accepting and *liking* are two completely different things. We can work to accept situations and people, but we may not *like* them.

A light bulb usually goes on when I say this to a patient. It is so much easier to accept something if it is at the same time okay to dislike it!

For example, I accept that my Uncle Henry is a rude and selfish man. I never expect that he will behave otherwise. When he is rude and selfish around me, I am not upset, because that's how he behaves. I don't take it personally because he is like this with everyone. It doesn't bother me because I accept it and no longer need to become outraged or indignant when he acts this way. Even though I have come to fully accept that this is how he behaves, I don't like it and try to spend less time in his company. I realize that his behavior is not a comment on me or a reflection of me. I will never change Uncle Henry; I can only change my degree of acceptance of him.

My only healthy choice is to align my view of him with the reality of him, not thinking and expecting he should be different. He can only be himself. With this way of seeing things, there is no "gap" between how things are and how I think they should be (previously known as my lack of acceptance) and I no longer suffer when I am around my uncle. It's fair to say that I don't like my uncle, but that fact doesn't cause me to suffer. Do you have an "Uncle Henry" in your life?

Align with What Is

There are a couple of important points to consider in the above example. The closer I align myself with *what is* and not with how I think things should be, the less I suffer. When I get out of the habit of interpreting others' behaviors as somehow being "about me," (i.e., Uncle Henry doesn't like me and that's why he is rude), I suffer less. When I wait for Uncle Henry to change so that the situation between us gets better, I give away my power and am a victim (i.e., believing that I can change nothing, but that when he becomes more civilized, I will then feel better). When I see my role in the dynamic (lack of acceptance) and take steps to shift my perspective, I change my degree of suffering to near zero.

I can be authentic with myself throughout this process, and don't need to tell myself a nonsense story to feel better (i.e., Uncle Henry is rude and insensitive, but that's okay, he doesn't really mean it). It's actually not okay that Uncle Henry is rude and selfish and I don't like it one bit. But I *accept* that he acts this way and I don't expect him to be any different when we are together. This is very clean and sits easily, with no suffering.

Let me illustrate this further with a few good examples from my practice.

Wanting More from Mom

Ellen, aged 36, came to see me after being diagnosed with a rare form of ovarian cancer. The operation to remove her ovaries and uterus went well, but she was devastated, as her dream of having children was crushed. She felt enormous grief.

Ellen was very overweight and during our initial interview told me her story. She has three siblings, none of whom talk to their mom. They all feel their mom is crazy and toxic. Ellen feels bad for her mom and feels too guilty to cut off ties with her, even though she acknowledges that her mom contributes greatly to the stress in her life. "I'm the only one she has left," she told me. Her mother is an unhappy person, who is pessimistic and critical. She has been critical of Ellen since she was a little girl. As a result, Ellen has internalized this and has a very low opinion of herself.

Ellen realizes her low self-esteem is due to her relationship with her mom, who has only become more negative and critical over the years. Ellen still tries to convince her mom that she is a good person, a smart person, and a worthy person by telling her mom stories and examples of her accomplishments at work and in her life.

When her mom needs help, she calls Ellen, who goes way out of her way to help her, still longing for the love and acknowledgement that she never gets. But her mom seems incapable of giving it. In our sessions, Ellen saw all this, but felt stuck as to what to do about it.

Underneath it all, Ellen was waiting for her mom to have an "ah-ha" moment and finally realize Ellen's true value and worth. Ellen was doing everything right and being a good girl, waiting for her mom to finally approve of her and show her love. But she had made herself sick with the stress of not being able to win her mother over, and trying harder and doing more had not worked. Her wasted efforts had only made her bitter, cynical and angry – how could her mom not see her for who she really was?

How do we even start to heal this problem?

First, we start with *acceptance of reality*. Ellen's mom is a self-centered and critical person who doesn't know how to show love to her kids. Very possibly, she herself was not well-loved as a child and never learned how to demonstrate love to others. We'll never know for sure. Ellen needs to deeply accept this fact and not continue to look for something from her mother that her mother doesn't have and therefore will never be able to give. Each time she comes up empty-handed, she goes back and tries harder to get something she will never get, and then becomes more bitter and angry. "Look at all I did for you, and you *still* can't love me?" It can be unbearably hard sometimes to see other people as they are, and accept them. But it is imperative if we want to stop the suffering.

As a wise teacher of mine once said: Don't go to the hardware store for bread. They don't sell it there. You might go once, thinking that they have it, and you are told, sorry we don't carry bread here. You might even go a second time, thinking they may have been out of stock the first time, only to come up empty-handed once again. But if you go a third time to the hardware store looking for bread, there is a serious problem of non-comprehension: *They don't sell bread at the hardware store!*

Ellen's mom doesn't have love to give Ellen. She might absolutely love Ellen but simply be unable to express it. Yes, that is sad and heartbreaking because mothers "should" love their children and be able to show it in a positive and affirming way, right? But that is not the reality in this case. And unless Ellen can see reality and accept it, her suffering (and possibly her health problems) will continue. She doesn't have to *like* the situation and she doesn't even have to like her mom, but she has to accept, accept, accept in order to move forward. Waiting for her mom to "get it" keeps her stuck and a victim of her mom's limitations.

I worked with Ellen to identify the limiting beliefs she had, and to change them. Through this Ellen was able to love herself and realize her own value and worth. She realized that she is a good person... and worthy of love. She realized her mom as the narcissist that she is. She decided to keep a relationship with her mom, but now on her terms. If her mom called her because she needed something, previously she would have run over to her mom's house to try to prove to her that she was a responsive daughter worthy of her mom's love. Now, she goes when she can, sometimes scheduling the date for the following week if she is busy.

Now Ellen shows up for her mom, not because she is trying to get love, but because it's a value she has. Knowing inside herself that she is a good and lovable person, allows her to set boundaries with her mom. She is no longer trying to exchange love for favors. My, what a difference! Accepting her mom as she is, she no longer suffers. She never expects her mom to show up any differently than she does. In fact, Ellen waits for her mom's predictably selfish comments and behaviors and chuckles to herself as soon as her mom delivers – her mom rarely disappoints in this regard!

Ellen has come to truly understand that this is simply the

way her mom is and it is not because of a deficit in *her*. What a change in perspective! By making changes in herself and in the way she sees the situation, she owns her role in the dysfunctional dynamic that existed between them and no longer feels bitter and angry around her mom. Further, she has proceeded to lose 30 pounds and is exercising and eating better than ever. Her cancer is behind her, she has asked her boyfriend of 15 years to marry her, and they are looking at adoption as a possibility. The changes she has made in her relationship with her mom has spread to other areas of her life: she doesn't take shit from other people anymore, as she is fond of saying, and goes after what she wants.

Trying to Manage the Unmanageable

Tommy, 38, came to me with the chief complaint of insomnia. Each night it would take him a long time to fall asleep; finally he would sleep for a few hours, only to wake around 3 a.m. Then worries about the day with work and family would intrude, making it difficult to fall back to sleep again. He tried over-the-counter sleep meds, which didn't help, and then prescription meds that made him groggy the next day. He came to me when he realized the better way forward was to deal with the *cause* of the problem – his stress and worry.

We started talking about his job. He had a very interesting job that made good use of his skills and talents as a transportation analyst, where he was responsible for getting goods from point A to point B, often in emergency and high stakes situations. He worked directly for the owner of the company, who was a visionary without a very practical approach to the business. The owner had surrounded himself with four excellent people on his management team, who were very skillful at their jobs, of which Tommy was one. But yet the company was having financial challenges.

Tommy really loved his work and the values of the company.

But he talked to me about his frustration with his boss who usually made emotional, off the cuff decisions to resolve problems. Tommy would present a proposal that he had thoroughly researched to arrive at the best, most cost-effective recommendations. His boss, who usually knew how he wanted to move forward based on his "gut feelings" before even hearing others' thoughts, always listened patiently, and then proceeded to do what he wanted, which often made little sense from a business perspective. Then predictably, after the boss' idea was implemented, the results were less than ideal, and cleaning up the mess cost additional money. Tommy often found himself in a position to repair already strained relationships with suppliers and stakeholders.

Tommy was extremely frustrated. He felt his boss did not value his opinion or see his hard work. He was angry that he had to repeatedly go and fix things up after the bad decisions his boss made, which were often the opposite of what Tommy had recommended. Other people on the management team were equally frustrated.

He did not want to quit the job as he valued his relationships there and was quite well paid. He told himself if he just worked harder to convince his boss to see things more clearly, things would get better. But in four years that had not yet happened. He came to work each day with good intentions, and pushed his agenda with his boss for the betterment of the projects he was working on. He had excellent relationships within the organization that made it all that much harder when he had to go back to colleagues and suppliers and explain why things were being done in a way that often appeared to make no sense. He would worry about it all night and be exhausted in the morning.

What to do? Lying there sleeplessly, Tommy would tell himself to stop worrying, that he didn't even own the business. That somehow things would work out, that all the problems would still be there tomorrow, so he could put them aside for the night.

The problem, we discovered, was that Tommy was unable to see and accept reality. Reality looked more like this: the owner of the company liked to do what he wanted to do regarding decisions in his company. He "pretended" to listen to Tommy's (and others') recommendations about issues, but trusted his gut and moved forward more or less regardless of what anyone had to say. He repeatedly made bad and costly decisions and still this did not motivate him to change his style. He didn't seem to link the financial struggles of the company with the poor decisions he had made.

Tommy was operating under the belief that his boss actually wanted to hear his analysis and was interested in his logical recommendations, but in all honesty this was not true and had never been true. His boss was determined to do things as he felt to do them, regardless of whatever analysis Tommy presented.

If Tommy could redefine his expectations of his role at the company, he would let go of a lot of the stress, be less disappointed each day, and possibly one day decide to move on to another opportunity which might offer him more satisfaction. It was hard to admit to himself that his real job was better described as: to simply give his well-researched opinion on various matters, and clean up the mess with staff and suppliers after his boss made poor, emotional decisions. He was not, as he had previously thought, there to drive decisions based on well-researched strategy or execute his own recommendations. Decisions were solely in the domain of his boss.

Because he had been under the misimpression that he was a player in the decision-making in the company, his stress and frustration were extremely high when he was not able to execute this role. To irritate things further, a lot of his time and energy went into work that his boss did not see or value, and which was, in the end, ignored.

Tommy fell into this trap every time he thought his boss

would react better to a new set of data or analysis he presented. Because he could not understand how anyone would make irrational, emotional decisions in the face of hard data, he could not see and accept his boss as he actually was. When he was finally able to see the situation accurately and accept it, he was able to find some peace. "My job is to make recommendations to someone who already knows how he wants to do things, and as such, my analysis, regardless of how great or persuasive, has little ability to influence him. My real job is running a cleanup operation to manage the fallout from his bad decisions, and limit their impact."

If I recently moved to Seattle from New Mexico and opened my curtains each morning in winter and became upset day after day that it was cloudy and raining, I'm sure Tommy would say to me, "Why are you upset, this is the weather in Seattle!" "Yes," I might say, "but *every* day? Surely, there should at least be *some* sunny days!" When I expect life to show up other than it does, and I do so day after day despite evidence to the contrary, my frustration and anger will have no end.

We may not like reality, but we must start with seeing it if we want to reclaim our emotional health. Of course, once we see things as they are, we have options. At the end of our discussion, Tommy had two pieces of clarity he didn't have previously: his revised job description based on reality, and a realization that the only way forward was to unite the other three members of the management team, who shared the same frustrations, to try to better manage their boss, rather than battling with him one on one as they each had been doing. He decided if that was not achieved within a one-year timeframe, he would consider leaving the job for more fulfilling work where his talents would be better utilized and recognized.

See what is true, accept what is true. With that clarity, find peace and possibly make different decisions, *Or not*, but at least you know where you stand, what reality tastes like. You are no longer living in denial, with the anger that always accompanies it.

I'm Stuck

Sue, 52, came to see me with depression. She felt stuck in a marriage of 20 years, angry all the time at her husband. He was a person totally absorbed by his work. It was his passion. He was a lawyer, and he lived and breathed the law. He saw everything in life from this analytical perspective. He was 100% there for his clients and worked most evenings and often on the weekends. He was a teacher at the local university and spent hours preparing lectures. He read books and articles on law. He was in the middle of writing two law books. Most every reference he made, even at the dinner table with his family, was often related in some way to law, or his work, or his cases.

He had wooed Sue passionately during their courtship, so she felt hurt and deceived by his shift in focus after their marriage. She felt she was somehow not enough, not interesting enough, to compete with his favorite subject. She felt like the mistress, the second priority. She felt unloved, not valued, not seen. She was angry because she had tried so hard to get his attention, and yet nothing had changed through the years.

When they had been dating he seemed interested enough: he wrote love letters and sent flowers. What had happened? The angrier she got, the more he instinctively moved away from her. The unhappier she seemed, the more he immersed himself in his work, where he was valued and esteemed by his clients and students for his knowledge and professional acumen.

When they had kids, Sue cut her work hours so she could be a more present mom. She took over most of the care, entertainment and raising of the kids, as it seemed her husband had "more important things" to do. The bitterness and resentment grew with the increased responsibility and workload of the kids. She considered leaving many times, but splitting up the family was not very appealing to her either. She felt totally stuck.

She *was* stuck: in non-acceptance of reality. In her mind her sentences about her husband often started with: "how could he... or, it's not right that he..." For her, she just couldn't understand how a parent would seemingly care more about his clients than his family... how it seemed he was happy to let her manage everything with the kids, go to every recital, deal with every decision and problem, attend all the teacher meetings – wasn't he interested? She viewed this as not fair, not right, and she was infuriated. Two years of couple's therapy didn't yield much change, though possibly a greater understanding of the problems. She lost respect for him and their marriage slowly disintegrated. Yet, she was still going through the motions, not wanting to break up the family.

Of course, we can see by now that Sue thought reality should be different than it was. And that belief caused her misery.

It was as if her husband was 5'6" but she thought he should be 5'9". She was furious that he was not 5'9" – but does that make any sense? Would anyone be furious with someone for his height? It's his height, we would say, what can he do about it? It's the way he is, the way he grew! We can't expect he will now simply grow to be 5'9" because that's the height you would prefer!

It took a while for the nickel to drop as Sue was so invested in her story of right and wrong. After all, shouldn't he do and say the things that a husband and father should if he loved and cared about their family? Sure, but he's only 5'6"! He only has the capacity to be the way he is. Every time Sue had the thought that her husband should be different than he was, she was miserable. She needed to see and begin to accept him exactly as he was. (Remember, this does not require that she "like" him or the situation.)

Once she finally *got* that this was him and he wasn't changing, she was no longer so angry. She made it a point to continuously align herself with reality – to expect him to show up just as he was: 5'6". And guess what? He never disappointed – he was never 5'9"! Her expectations were now more in line with reality and her suffering was greatly diminished.

Sue realized that she had two healthy choices: accept him as he was and make peace with the good things he brought to the marriage (financial stability, reliability, some limited amount of attentiveness, etc.) or leave and try to find more fulfillment with another person. While she was still in the process of making that decision when last we spoke, she is much happier as a person and has moved on from the continuous argument in her mind of how he should be compared to how he is.

Dealing with Disappointment

An old patient, Merrill, came to see me when she heard I was doing this work of "repatterning" emotions. She came because she wanted to see if she could get over her resistance to getting her business to a new level. She had been working at it for seven years, and they had achieved some mild success, enough to pay the bills with a little left over. But she was tired of working so hard and still feeling like she was struggling financially. Despite that, she was reluctant to really put in all it would take to blast her business off through the roof.

In our discussion, she quickly revealed that she was afraid of being disappointed. What if she put everything she had into it... and it didn't grow? Or, it did go through the roof and then it failed – they lost a major account, or they were sued... the more you have, the more you have to lose, you know! She felt like she couldn't take any more disappointment in her life.

So I asked her what else had disappointed her. Her husband had left after 20 years of marriage. It wasn't a great marriage but she had never pictured herself divorced, or getting older alone. I asked her what else had disappointed her. And then her eyes teared up. Her daughter had been diagnosed with severe arthritis as a child. She was now in her early twenties and living a full life, but in chronic pain and on full time heavy-duty medication to manage the symptoms. Her son had quit school just before graduating college and seemed lost, with no plans for the future. She had recently met a guy who she cares deeply about, but he lives six hours from her and they only got to see each other occasionally.

Her capacity to tolerate more disappointment than what she was already living was about zero. How could she possibly take a business risk?

As we dug down deeper, it became apparent that the disappointment was because Merrill felt that things shouldn't be the way they were. Her husband should not have left because, though things were not great, he should have had the same commitment to marriage that she had. Her daughter should not have arthritis, why should such a beautiful girl suffer for nothing? Her son should have finished school, as he was just a few months from graduating when he quit, and should somehow be moving forward with his life like all his friends were doing. Her boyfriend was a light in her life, but it was disappointing that he couldn't be more there for her with the distance separating them.

Carefully, I made the suggestion that she had not accepted the reality of her life and that her resistance to it was equal to her disappointment. As a result, she had pitched her tent in the house of disappointment and was now living there. She had masked this quite well. Maybe aside from a few close friends, no one knew that underneath her happy, joking exterior was a person in deep pain.

No shocker: Merrill did not want to hear this. Acceptance? How could I possibly accept any of this? Accepting this would be condoning it. I don't condone any of it. It should all be different than it is – I should still be married, my daughter should be well, my son should have his life together and still be in school etc. Really?

It was a delicate situation. How could I possibly propose to Merrill that things were exactly how they "should" be, simply because that's how they *are*? There was nothing right about what she was living, as she saw it, and to propose that to her was almost an insult.

So, I asked her... "What is your belief system? Why do you think we are here, on planet Earth?" She said, "To learn and grow." She quickly added that she wasn't sure about reincarnation, but she did believe that the soul of the person still lives after death.

So I asked her, "How do you think we learn and grow?" She paused, beginning to see the kind of "trap" I was laying. Merrill is no dummy. Is it possible that your daughter is exactly where she needs to be? That she came here to learn and her illness provides her the opportunity to experience exactly what she needs in order to evolve? And that this is between her and the Universe? And that we would never want to deprive her of her learning, or in any way alter her path. That it is her life, in co-creation with the Universe? Sadly, as her mother, Merrill has the worst seat in the house, front and center. There is nothing equal to a mother's suffering for her child, as I well know.

Merrill said, what could she possibly learn from this illness, from being sick, in pain and not living a "normal" life?

I suggested a few possibilities: to dig deep when she is not feeling well and find the strength to go to her classes, take her exams, go to a friend's party that she was looking forward to, despite feeling sick that day? To develop sympathy and compassion for all those who are suffering, and who have to make the best of things each day, despite enormous pain? To learn to be available to help others who are struggling, the way family, friends and health professionals have shown up for her? Isn't this learning? Isn't this growing and evolving? Who are we to say the lessons should be taught differently than how they are being taught?

Merrill was thoughtful. A paradigm shift was happening, but she was still struggling with the word acceptance. "So, that's it, then? We just accept that she has this disease and find a way to make ourselves okay with it?" "No!" I said, "You fight like hell to make things better." Accept does not mean you pull out the lounge chair and make yourself a pina colada. It means you accept *the challenge*. You don't argue with the method of teaching or the lesson being taught. You accept that it was given to you and then you give everything you have to go through it as well as possible. This is where the growth and evolution take place. Not in putting up your tent (or worse, building a house) in the land of disappointment because things shouldn't be this way. Things *are* this way. The only question is, how can we best accept this and show up for it... knowing that there's something in it for us, or we wouldn't be living it?

Challenge

Are there people or situations in your life who you have trouble accepting as is? I would wager there are many! With which of these people or situations does your non-acceptance cause you to suffer the most? That's the best place to start with this work! In what ways do you have a lack of acceptance of them or their behavior? How can you adjust the situation in your mind so that you can see it simply as it is, and not expect it to be different? It's much easier to shift our view than to change others!

I find acceptance to be one of the hardest things for people to do. Our default mode is: things shouldn't be this way! My son should do better in school, my daughter should not have an eating disorder, my husband should not be working all the time, my mother should take more of an interest.

Every time we are able to neutralize our disharmony with life and move toward acceptance, we find greater peace.

Chapter 4

Responsibility

Assume as much of it as we can to increase our sphere of influence...

In any problem between you and another, with any situation from the past that haunts you, I recommend that you try to see your part in it and take as much responsibility for the problem as possible.

Now please don't hang up!

Most of us do a pretty good business in blame. It is so much easier to tell the story with the other guy being the wrongdoer. In any fight we've had with another, in any broken relationship, in any discord, it is human nature to dramatize the wrongdoings of the other, and see ourselves as the one being taken advantage of, the underdog.

I propose to you that this way of seeing events keeps us small, limits our growth and evolution, and ultimately, our happiness.

When we look back on the past, or even on our ongoing problems, it's by taking as much responsibility as possible that we have the power to change the dynamic and change ourselves. If it's all the other person's fault, and we are the victim, we can change little. We were wronged, we were screwed-over, and that's the end of the story – poor us. But when we had a role to play in the dynamic, and if we can be super-honest, maybe even a big role, then we take our power back by owning it.

We can say to ourselves, objectively, without self-punishment: "Wow, I kind of screwed up there." By admitting that to ourselves, we open the door to learning something. That learning makes us realize that we want to show up better next time. That is real growth and evolution. That is power. That is self-mastery. The other option, denial, blaming and shirking responsibility, offers no learning and no growth, and we are bound to repeat the same situations again and again. Sure, it feels better to see things as the fault of the other, then we are blameless. It hurts so much to be wrong! But there is no growth down that path.

Loving-Kindness and Hindsight

Sheila, aged 45, came to see me suffering with anxiety. She was crying all the time. She felt very bad about her life. A lot of difficult things had happened to her. And now her kids were growing up and moving out, her husband was busy with his work, and she had "nothing." She felt worthless, that she had no skills and nothing of value to occupy herself.

The problems all started a few years earlier when her family moved into a house that she never really liked, which then turned out to be full of mold. She got sick and became exhausted, debilitated and depressed.

This is the way she told me the story: her family had been living in an apartment that her brother-in-law owned, and were paying him rent. The situation worked well, they enjoyed the apartment and it suited their needs perfectly. Then her brother-in-law suggested that maybe they should purchase a home for their growing family. Sheila was actually not interested in moving and was very happy where they were. But her husband thought it was a good idea.

Sheila felt that her husband and his brother knew best, so they started looking for a house and found one that her husband really liked but that she didn't care for. But she went along with her husband so as to not rock the boat. Six months after moving in, she started feeling sick and when they tested the house they found there was mold coming from the basement of their attached neighbor. As much as they tried, they had limited influence in getting their 70-year-old neighbor to spend the money to clean up the problem.

That was 10 years ago. A few years into the problem, Sheila

became very depressed. She hated the house and regretted ever moving in the first place. Her sister advised her to see a therapist, and recommended one whom she had heard good things about. She met the therapist and he suggested she go on anti-depressants. She didn't like the idea of going on medication, but he was the doctor and probably knew best so she started taking them. The meds made her feel lethargic. During the course of the therapy, the therapist sexually molested her. Each time she would go to see him, he would touch her inappropriately, telling her how attracted he was to her. She felt like too much of a zombie on the medication to do or say anything about it and continued going to see him, hating herself the whole time.

As she sat in my office crying, and telling me about the unfolding of the last few years, it was clear she had a lot of anger, resentment and shame. She was angry with her brother-in-law for suggesting they move in the first place. How dare he act like he knew what was best for them? It was because of him that they bought the house that caused her to get sick with mold poisoning. Then she was angry with her husband. She had intimated to her husband they she wasn't crazy about the house while they were shopping around, but he pushed on with it despite her criticisms and now they were stuck with it. She was angry with her sister for recommending a therapist who put her on strong medications that had made her into a zombie (she was now off them) and furious at the therapist who had used his professional status to abuse her trust. She knew she shouldn't have kept going back, but she felt she was under his spell. She was so desperate for help, she was willing to follow whatever he suggested in order to feel better. She felt guilty and ashamed, hopeless and pessimistic that anything could ever get better for her.

Listening to her story, I was struck by the amount of blaming and the lack of responsibility Sheila took for the way her life had turned out. If she would be able to see that and take responsibility for the ways she had failed herself, she would be able to move forward, feeling empowered and ready to face the next chapter of her life. It became clear through our discussions that her deep need to be loved was behind her need to please others at any cost (even the therapist who was abusing her) and her pattern of putting herself and her own needs last overpowered her good judgment about what was right for her.

The past is gone. What's the point of dwelling on it? Hanging on to a story that we created about events that makes us miserable is not a way to live. The past really *is* gone. Let's turn the page, take the "key learnings" we got from it, and apply them forward to create a better future for ourselves. Dwelling on what makes us powerless yields more of the same. All we have is today and what we create from now forward.

I coached Sheila through the re-telling of her story in order to take full responsibility for the moments when she could have better advocated for herself. The point of the exercise was not to make her feel worse by pointing a finger at her mistakes. Rather for her to take as much responsibility for the difficult parts in her story as she could, so she could see where she had failed herself, learn from it and move on in a better way. If everything is always everybody else's fault, how can we ever learn – except to learn to trust no one?

Here's the re-write we created: When her brother-in-law suggested that they find a new house, Sheila could have spoken up and said, "We appreciate your concern for us, but actually we like this apartment very much and we'd like to stay here for the time being. We feel no need to move, thank you." Had they decided to move, and her husband was starting to get serious about a house she wasn't interested in, she could have spoken clearly and said, "I'm not happy with this house, I'd like to take if off the list of possibilities." When she didn't feel good on the medications she might have decided to get off them. Once she realized that she was not in a healthy situation with the therapist, she could have trusted her instincts, canceled her appointments and reported his abuse right away.

Of course, this is all easy to see in hindsight. What is clear, though, is that at every turn, Sheila gave her power away to those who she decided knew what she needed better than she did herself. By not taking ownership of this, it was impossible for her to be confident in moving forward to create a better future. By continuing to blame everyone involved without looking at her own responsibility in her situation, she ensures that she will continue the pattern of staying small and not speaking up for herself.

Sometimes it's hard to look back at where we've gone wrong and own it. I helped Sheila look at her actions with loving-kindness and see where she might have stood up for herself more effectively. We discussed at length that it's unfair to look back at the past with self-criticism; we have to give ourselves the benefit of the doubt: acknowledging that we did the best we could with what we knew – and the skills we had – in the moment. Of course, years later and with more wisdom, it's sometimes easy to look back and wonder why we didn't make better decisions. But back then, we didn't have the clarity that hindsight affords us now.

By trying to take as much responsibility as possible for everything that had unfolded in the last 10 years, Sheila gained a sense of stature and power. She gained self-respect. She could see where she had let herself down, learn from it and resolve to move forward with more consciousness to know herself and her needs, and speak up for herself in matters of consequence to her. And that realization was the beginning of her healing.

She forgave herself for the past and was able to start to let go of the hold it had over her. She started volunteering and then got a part-time job. It felt good to earn money and take on extra responsibility. And at her insistence, her husband finally agreed to put their house up for sale.

Afraid of Being Alone

Robert, a man in his mid-forties, had been a patient of mine for many years. I had treated him for a variety of ailments over time, including sciatica. He was married with a small daughter. I was treating him with homeopathy on one occasion for a recurrent flare up of his sciatica, and one thing became quite obvious to me – his sciatica always became worse when he got very angry or stressed. He came limping into my office one afternoon, with a look of pain written all over his face.

He said, "My wife wants to separate. I think she is interested in another man." He went on to describe that his wife told him she felt they had grown apart and no longer had much in common. They hadn't been intimate in over a year and she was no longer interested in being close to him on any level. She had moved into the spare bedroom.

Whatever she asked of him, he did, as he was afraid he would further risk losing her if he didn't acquiesce. She started going out in the evenings and coming back late, but Robert said nothing. She told him he was boring and she no longer felt close to him, and he tried harder. He made her favorite dinner, brought her flowers. The more she pulled away, the more frantically he tried to please her. The more he tried, the more respect she lost for him. By the time he came to see me his sciatica was hurting 24/7. But as we spoke, all I could see was how boiling mad he was. "After all I've done for her, after all I've put up with, she still wants to leave me," he reported in a quiet voice. I did this for her and I did that for her...

As we started to talk more deeply, it became clear what he himself had not even realized: that he wanted her to stay, not because he was so in love with her, and not because he himself was so happy in the marriage, but because underneath it all, he had a terrible fear of being alone.

We traced this fear to his childhood in Russia, where his mother had been orphaned at a young age and had suffered greatly from feeling as if she didn't belong to anyone. She had raised Robert with the value of the importance of family so he would not suffer as she had.

As soon as Robert saw the connection, his whole understanding of the situation changed. He was honestly able to admit to himself that he was not happy in the marriage either, and that the desperation he felt to connect with his wife was not necessarily from love, but from fear of abandonment. This fear was a key underpinning of his relationship with her, which led him to lose himself in pleasing her, just so that she wouldn't leave.

This was obviously very boring for his wife, because she was married to simply a "yes" man: someone who didn't have his own opinions or ideas, someone who was afraid to rock the boat, to get into an argument, to reveal the interesting person that lived underneath the fear. In fact, Robert admitted to me that underneath the fear he himself had no idea who he was or what he wanted – he hadn't dared to ask. His subconscious priority had been to be likeable and agreeable so that he wouldn't ever be left alone. Ironically, it's this very fear that created the behaviors that would contribute to his being alone!

When he really looked at whether or not he was happy in the marriage, he had to admit that in recent years he had not been. When he was confronted with the question of whether he truly wanted to be married to someone who wasn't in love with him, and in fact, barely respected him, he admitted he didn't want that for himself. When he saw that his fear of being alone had driven so many of his decisions over the years, he was dumbfounded.

Taking responsibility for this was not an exercise in self-blame. But only through seeing it honestly was he able to own his part in the failure of the marriage. A healthy marriage is based on love, respect and shared interests, among other things, not on fear and the avoidance of loneliness, not as a prop to hide behind. And even though his wife didn't necessarily know any of this, surely she felt the lack of genuine connection.

We discussed that his wife actually had the most clarity of the two of them, and the courage to move out of a "safe" situation to find a more satisfying relationship. He agreed. He went home and apologized to his wife and told her he accepted the separation she was proposing. Within a few months he had met another woman at his workplace and they were developing a deep and rich connection, more authentic than he had ever experienced.

Seeing our role with honesty and clarity in any dynamic is liberating. It quickly dissolves anger, hatred, resentment into understanding and compassion for ourselves and the others involved. From this place of objectivity about our role in any dysfunction, we can see, we can learn, we can grow. And hopefully stop repeating the same patterns again and again! Clarity about our ourselves and our motives can be very hard to see objectively, but is essential if we are to change patterns and dynamics. If we simply try to change surface behaviors without digging deeper to the root cause of those behaviors, real change will be difficult.

Ask yourself honestly: what drives me to act this way? If you listen deeply and openly, unafraid to know the truth, the answers will be there.

Working with Forgiveness

Samantha, 35, had gone to see an astrologer who had come highly recommended by her aunt. She wanted to get more clarity about whether or not to move in with her boyfriend of two years. They loved each other a lot and had much in common. However, they fought frequently and the fights were getting more and more difficult to resolve without lingering pain.

Samantha was hurt because her boyfriend had a very rigid schedule during the week – work, working out and teaching yoga – which left little time for them to see each other. He frequently made what seemed like "selfish" decisions that didn't leave too much room for her. She felt as though he didn't care about her and this triggered her to feel very hurt and angry, which usually resulted in a big fight. With each blow up, the recovery was longer and wariness about the other lingered.

Fully expecting to hear from the astrologer, who looked at each of their charts separately and together, that it was not a good match, that her boyfriend was a self-centered person who didn't care enough about others, she was shocked when she was told that she had some work to do on herself!

The astrologer was able to see in her chart that she had a difficult relationship with her dad. In fact, her parents had divorced when she was 8 years old and her mom had moved 500 miles away with Samantha and her sister. The girls saw their dad only during summer vacations and at Christmas. Her mom moved in with her boyfriend, and her dad remarried and subsequently had two more children. She never felt quite as important to him as his new family seemed to be.

There were numerous examples over the 20-plus years of how her dad had not been there for her, how he had fallen short, how she had felt unloved and unimportant to him. While the astrologer couldn't know the details, he could clearly see the wound. He told her that each time it seemed to her that her boyfriend was not there for her 100%, it re-triggered the wound from her dad. She would feel hurt and would overreact to even very small things. Her feelings of being unloved and abandoned were never very far beneath the surface, and easily aroused.

Her boyfriend had become so afraid of her anger that he had closed down and was constantly afraid of triggering her. The astrologer told her she needed to take responsibility for her part in the story. The anger she was carrying toward her dad, and the deep grudge she had against him, was a block. Until she was able see that and take responsibility for forgiving him, *really forgiving* him, for all that she perceived he had done wrong, she would never heal. This was her work to do. And until she did this, that wound would be triggered again and again, leading to fighting and suffering in this relationship, and in future ones.

To her, all the neglect and hurtful things her dad had done, unintentional as they may have been, seemed *unforgivable*. How do you forgive when you can't really feel forgiveness? When the behaviors have hurt you so much that they are unforgivable?

You learn that forgiveness is for yourself, not for the other. The astrologer explained to her his view of things: "You chose your parents, Sam, and you chose this situation to learn and grow in this life. If you choose now to take responsibility for all the difficulties you faced, accept and forgive and move forward, your wounds will heal. You'll find happiness and peace in your relationships that can't possibly be there when you see all the actions of your boyfriend through the lens of hurt. Accepting your dad, and the situation, and realizing that everyone did the best they could with what they understood in the moment, is a release from *your* suffering."

Sam got it. She saw that taking responsibility for her part in the dynamic with her boyfriend, and showing up with courage to look inside and find what she needed to do – not how *he* needed to change – would empower her.

This was big. What had been her dad's fault and her boyfriend's fault was now resting squarely in her lap. If she took responsibility for forgiving her dad and communicating clearly and honestly with her boyfriend when she felt triggered, change would be almost assured.

If she didn't, she could see nothing would change. She vowed to move forward to change all that she could *for herself*. Regardless of whether she ended up with this guy or another, she knew she would never regret doing that work. The first step was owning her part.

Challenge

It seems like for so many of us, blame is the default mode. Why is it so painful, so awful, to see where *we* have contributed to our difficulties?

Maybe seeing our role in our problems awakens the shame in ourselves that lies buried in our subconscious beliefs, shame about our unlovability, or maybe our inherent lack of goodness? Wouldn't life be so much simpler if we could see our errors and not have it hurt so much? If we could do that, we would be able to ask ourselves right away and automatically, what might I have done better here? What could I do better now?

How much less complicated things would be if I could just see that, make the necessary adjustments and move on, without getting tangled up in blaming. If I could just fix my part in any dynamic, wouldn't things be just *that much better*? The other party may or may not ever improve their game, but taking care of my business is the piece that's mine alone to do... because it's never about the other person, anyway, right?

Chapter 5

Stories

The language we use and perspective we have about events in our lives reveal where we need to heal...

When patients tell me their stories, I am often struck by their recounting of them. Is any story really objective, simply based on the facts? It seems they are all told through our particular wounded lenses.

The stories we tell about what happened to us are subjective versions of the facts. They are told through our distortions. By no means are we "lying" or purposely telling the story in any particular way – our version is truly how we have experienced it, and how it gets recorded in our brains.

But once we realize that, actually, there are many truthful ways to describe the same set of facts, we realize we have a *choice* as to how we interpret our experiences. And the interpretation we pick reveals a lot about how we see the world, how we feel about ourselves and, importantly, results in the future that we create!

Consider this: if there was an elephant standing in the room between you and me, and I was standing at his head, and you were standing at his tail, and we were each asked to describe what we saw... our descriptions would be completely different! I would describe a long trunk that swayed back and forth, two ivory tusks, two eyes with long lashes, a large mouth, and two big floppy ears. You would describe a thin tail that swished in the air, and two very wide gray legs with lots of folds of skin, topped by two very large buttocks. Our descriptions would be *completely* different, yet we would both be telling the truth – it's the same elephant!

If we would both move a few steps to the left, we would describe something different yet again. A thing, an event, a relationship has many different accurate versions that can be used to describe it. And it's up to us to choose the version that we decide to assimilate as "truth." This version is revealed in the way we think about what happened and in the way we talk about it.

I often invite patients: can we tell ourselves a different and better version of the same facts? One that is equally true, but kinder to ourselves? One equally true, but where we are the hero, the smart one... rather than the victim? Not in any way to lie or tell ourselves a falsified story – we would never deeply believe it. But to actually tell ourselves an *equally true* but kinder interpretation of the same facts. *Why would we NOT choose the better version?*

The Stories We Tell

A few years ago, I had the pleasure of working with a 17-year-old girl I'll call Anne. She was very smart and very pretty, an overachiever – many friends, good at school. She was very well-adjusted, except in her home life. She had a very strained relationship with her dad, Alan.

Alan was a very successful and active business leader. He was heavily involved with his professional life and wasn't very attentive to her. He didn't show much interest in what she was doing, or her plans for the future. He never really tried to create one-on-one time with her, or to find common interests to develop their relationship. To make matters worse, he seemed to be more involved with her younger brother, Max, who was super-interested in sports – he played sports, he watched sports, he lived and breathed sports. Alan and Max had this in common, and talked about sports frequently, watching games together on TV and occasionally going out to sporting events. Seeing how her dad was more involved with her brother hurt Anne even more. His apparent disinterest in her felt even more personal.

I continued to see her occasionally through the years after she went away to college. Not once in that first year away did her dad phone or text her to find out how she was doing. He relied on getting that information from his wife, who was regularly in touch with Anne. This was confirmation for Anne that her dad didn't care about her. After all, if he had, he would have shown some interest. She admitted that in their limited interactions when she was home, she was not very nice or encouraging to him, because she was so hurt: she usually gave one-word answers to any questions he asked her. But still, she reasoned, he was the adult.

Alan, her dad, was raised as the fifth of seven kids. It was a busy house with Alan's dad working in the family grocery store and his mom plainly overwhelmed with all the children. Alan got lost in the crowd. There wasn't anyone very attentive to his needs during childhood, and rarely did anyone inquire about how he was doing. He learned to be self-sufficient and need little from others. In his adult life, he had very few friends to speak of. His relationship with his wife was strained for many of the same reasons as it was with their daughter. He was not a good communicator but was actually a very happy and contented person in himself.

He was a good person with a kind heart but without knowledge of how to connect on a deeper level with others. This was pointed out to him numerous times, but he had little interest in addressing the subject. Perhaps he didn't know how to fix it, but he seemed quite content with himself, according to Anne. He was running an extremely successful business, and invested more and more of his energy in that realm, opening numerous stores throughout the city.

I worked with Anne to help her tell herself a different story about her dad. The one she was telling herself was causing her so much suffering: my Dad doesn't love me, if he did he would show more of an interest in me. He would have made an effort to cultivate a relationship with me; after all, he's able to do that with people in his business, *and* with my brother. I am hurt and angry about this, because I don't know what I did wrong.

Yes, this is one version of the story. It feels true to Anne. But it is so very painful. The suffering is endless, because there is no way to make this problem better the way she tells the story – because Anne can never be more than she is in order to get her Dad's love and attention.

Anne and I created a new version, no less true than the first version, but far less painful. It went like this:

My dad has an injured part. That part got damaged in his own childhood because he was not raised with the love and attention he probably needed. It's hard to give what you never received. As a result, my Dad doesn't know how to connect with the majority of people. He has few friends and few close people in his life. He is closest to his partners and employees, where the relationship is more distant by definition, not intimate like in a family. My Dad's distance from me *is not personal*, not because of me or even about me. It feels personal at times, but I now realize that it has little to do with me. I am sad that I don't have a closer relationship with my Dad, it's a loss in my life, but I accept that my Dad is imperfect and I am not to blame. I hope at some point in my life, I can reach out to my Dad from a better place, with no hurt or anger, and accept him how he is, knowing that however he responds, it's not a reflection on me.

Why not tell ourselves a better version of our stories? Not just *tell* ourselves, but *believe* it deeply?

For me, it's like having a lot of clothes in your closet. Some are old, out of style, make you look fat and have a few stains on them. Others are more recently purchased, very flattering and you feeling amazing when you wear them. Which ones are you going to put on today? It's your choice. Why would we choose the clothes that make us feel terrible when we could choose the outfit that makes us feel beautiful?

Similarly, there are many interpretations of the facts: *none necessarily more real or right than the others*. Why choose the version that makes us feel bad, sad and suffer? The other, more neutral (or even beautiful) versions are hanging right next to that one. It's about recognizing that we have a choice, which possibly never occurred to us before.

Different Story, Same Facts

Another patient named Steve once told me a story that brilliantly illustrates this point. About 20 years ago, he was driving and his car hit an icy patch. He skidded off the road, hit the railing on the side and his car flipped over. A Fleetwood Mac song was playing at the time, which later became associated with the memory of those terrifying moments of losing control of the car. Miraculously, he was unharmed. An ambulance arrived on the scene and he was taken to the nearest hospital. Besides a gash on his head that needed a few stitches, he was in fine shape.

But interestingly, every time he heard Fleetwood Mac on the radio, he winced and couldn't turn the dial fast enough to change the station or skip the song. The music was a reminder of the terror he felt as his car was going off the road.

He was telling this story to a friend of his one day, and the friend had a most interesting reply. He said, "Steve, I find it so astonishing that you hate to listen to Fleetwood Mac. If it were me, I would go out of my way to play their music! That's the group associated with your survival against all odds! You should have been dead from your car flipping over, or at least, paralyzed with a broken neck. How you survived that fate is a miracle! That song should be your theme song about your ability to survive in this world, and thrive!"

Wow – different interpretation, same facts. One positive and inspiring, one negative and fear-based.

Too Burnt Out to Continue

A long-time patient of mine who, for the last 20 years, ran and managed her own advertising company, came in to see me last May, devastated. She was burnt out, exhausted and out of juice. She was running on fumes. But that's not why she was upset. Her business, which had always had its ups and downs, was facing a serious slump. There were no campaigns or activities scheduled for the next three months. She was in a total panic. "What am I going to do with myself, where is the money going to come from? Is this the beginning of the end?" she lamented. "I've put my life into that business… is this what I have to show for it?" Then, in the next second she said, "I can't do this anymore, I'm too tired. I can't face another day at that office."

I said to her, "Pina, why don't you take the summer off? You have nothing planned anyway and all you are saying to me is how burnt out you are. You need to *refuel, reenergize, recreate.* When's the last time that you took a real break? Got your creative juices flowing again? Is it possible that this 3-month space before you was custom made for you to do just that?"

She looked at me, slightly baffled. "I can't be away from the office for three whole months!" "Why not?" I asked, "You have no work anyway!" "Really? I can?" she asked. "Not only can you, you must. What choice do you have – you are too burnt out to contribute much anyway, right?" She left my office in a daze and I didn't hear from her for almost two months.

When she came back in to see me, she looked amazing, with a great tan and a radiant smile. "Thank you," she said, "you literally saved my life. I did just what you said, I rested and read. I went away for a week to a writing workshop. I made a list of what I'm good at and what I love and I will create more of that in my life going forward. These last couple of months were the best thing that ever happened to me. I can't believe I have only one month left – I am treasuring each minute and hope it goes slowly."

Now that's what I call a change of perspective! The facts were the same: no projects on the table for three whole months. No cash flow coming in. One perspective: this is the worst thing that could ever happen... after all I've worked for, how can I face this insult? Even though I'm burnt out, I need to keep pushing to grind out a living. Another perspective: this 3-month space has appeared. The timing is perfect as I am so tired and in need of rest. I will take the time with the goal of refueling, re-evaluating my priorities and re-calibrating where I want to go over the next few months and years. I've worked so hard this year and I need the rest to get my creative juices flowing again!

Wow – what a different spin on the same thing! Can you see that our interpretation of what happens is more important than the facts? What kinds of stories are we telling ourselves in our running narrative of the world that distorts the way we see things and causes us to suffer? What story can we retell ourselves about something that is causing us pain, and see it differently? If there are many valid interpretations of the facts, why wouldn't we choose the one that is kindest and gentlest to ourselves? Seriously! Life is hard enough!

Banishing Shame

Speaking of hard enough, it has been very humbling during my years of working with people to work with women who have been sexually abused. The stories range from moderate, inappropriate touching on a one-time basis, to repeated overt invasion by a "trusted" family member over many years. These events are almost as hard to hear as they are to reveal.

While by all means the emotional effects of such tyranny are complicated, in almost all cases my patients report an over-riding feeling of shame.

I'll share one patient's story in particular, where re-writing her story together helped her move past the shame.

Essie was in her forties and raised in a Hassidic religious

Jewish community. When she was 18 years old, her parents started inquiring around for a husband for her. Since boys and girls are largely separated until that age, parents are relied upon to make the match. Her parents introduced Essie to Jacob and they had a few short dates to get to know each other, which was customary. They liked each other and agreed to be married.

They married a few months later and moved to France where her husband had a business and Essie became pregnant within a few months. During the pregnancy, Jacob started making unkind remarks to her about how she looked. Of course she was hurt, but tried to overlook it. After the baby was born, the negative comments and criticism increased. Essie was sad and very unhappy, but as Jacob seemed very volatile, she decided to try to ignore it and not make matters worse by confronting him. Time went on, the comments became pinches and slaps and forced, violent sex.

Essie knew things were very wrong but felt she had nowhere to turn. Her husband was terribly critical and insulting, telling her every day that she was fat and stupid. She began to believe him, which kept her more paralyzed.

Divorce is very much frowned upon in their community so Essie did everything possible to try to accommodate Jacob's erratic and violent outbursts so as not to have to separate from him. Whenever she thought of telling someone, she felt terribly ashamed and that somehow it was all her fault, and that kept her silent. At one point she confided to her father in a phone call about how unhappy she was and her dad didn't seem to hear her cry for help. He went on to reassure her that marriage has its ups and downs and she needed to ride it through.

The second child came and the abuse got worse. By this point, Essie had such a low opinion of herself she didn't think it was even possible to experience happiness. Her husband was a skillful manipulator and a bully. He sexually abused her on a regular basis.

Finally, one day, she had the opportunity to confide in her mom who was visiting from the States. Immediately understanding the severity of the situation, she brought Essie and her two sons back home with her that same week.

After living at her parents' house for a few years and seeing a therapist to try to recover from her four years in that marriage, Essie felt better. She was once again introduced by her parents to a potential mate, a man also divorced with two kids. They agreed it would be a good match and are now married with a new baby of their own.

This is the point in the story where I met Essie. Her oldest son from her first marriage had just gotten engaged. Her ex-husband Jacob, who had also moved back to the States from France, had gotten wind of the engagement and wanted to be reacquainted with their son. The boy wanted nothing to do with his father whom he had not seen in almost 20 years, but Essie was terrified because Jacob was back in the picture, sniffing around them. It brought her right back to how she felt about herself in that marriage: small, incapable, terrified, victim-like and ashamed. She wanted to learn how to stop hearing those terrible thoughts in her head.

I've never seen the "sweep the garbage under the rug, close and lock the door and pretend that room doesn't exist in my house" strategy work. Yet we all want to do it on occasion. Instead, I'm a big fan of the "open all the windows and turn on the lights, sweep up all the garbage including the dust bunnies hiding in the corners, sift through it for any pearls of wisdom and discard the rest" strategy, leaving the door to the room open to make sure it's fully aired out and integrated as part of the household.

Maybe that sounds difficult, but I can assure you in the end, it's the easier approach. Because the dirt under the carpet in the room with no air is where things start to rot. And the rot seeps into the surrounding rooms and ultimately into the foundations of the house. And when that happens the tentacles of rot are so far-reaching that it's much harder to eradicate.

What does it take? Courage, and a willingness to re-write the story you told yourself.

Essie agreed. We held hands (figuratively speaking), and went into that locked room together. We peeled back the rug and turned on all the lights. We saw the facts of the story. A young and naïve girl in a foreign country. A man whom she was dependent on for her safety and basic needs. A culture where divorce was a public humiliation and actively discouraged. Two small children whose family she would be breaking apart if she left. No one locally to confide in, her family being very far away. Her fear of Jacob further injuring her if she confronted the situation more directly.

Then: her courage to come forward and tell her mom, rather than continue to pretend, her courage to leave with her boys and go into therapy to try to heal, her courage to marry again and give life another try.

I asked her to tell me exactly which part of the story caused her to feel ashamed. She answered, "That it even happened. That I stayed there and let it continue to happen."

"Could you have prevented it from happening?" "No." "Could you have known in advance it was going to happen, with what you knew of him?" "No." "Given the facts we laid out, isn't it obvious that at each moment you did what you thought was best, trying to accommodate an impossible situation where there was no obvious good outcome?" "Yes."

So, why the shame? Which of your behaviors do you feel ashamed of? "I know," Essie said, "but why did it take so long? If I had valued myself more, I should have left immediately."

I explained the analogy of the frog in a saucepan of water. If you put a frog in a pan with some cold water in it, the frog will happily play there. When you turn the fire on to simmer, the water gradually heats up, but because the increase in temperature is gradual, the frog never realizes it should jump out. Each degree hotter is only a little bit hotter than previously, so the frog continues to hop around. At a certain point, the water starts to boil and cooks the frog. On the other hand, if you put a frog in a pot of already hot water it will do its best to jump out immediately.

In Essie's case, the abuse got gradually worse and worse and it was hard for her to appreciate how bad things had gotten. If on the first night of her marriage her husband had acted how he acted at the end, there's no doubt in her mind that she would have left immediately.

For me, the take home point was that she *did* get out. She saved herself and her boys. It took the time it took. It took the opportunity of her mom's visit. But she did it. So, could she re-write the story to one of how proud she was of herself: having tried to deal with a horrible situation as best as she could, and then when it was no longer tolerable, she reached for help and changed her life.

We feel ashamed when we feel we have done something wrong and we are the guilty party. Isn't it actually astonishing that so many victims of sexual abuse are the ones to feel the shame? Is it possible to re-write the story to one of pride and courage? A survival story? Because at the end of the day, *you got yourself out*, you survived it.

How unfair now to look back once the water is boiling and say, I should have gotten out sooner. As the water was barely heating up, it was impossible to know that it was headed for a full boil.

Together, Essie and I re-wrote her story so it became about her intelligence, resourcefulness and courage. We acknowledged her ability to heal and her willingness to try again and find happiness for herself. We agreed that she could walk tall, proudly even, wearing the scars from life like a badge of honor on her sleeve, for all she had lived through and was victorious over.

Wow, was that a turnaround for Essie. Finally, we discussed that if a girlfriend had shared a similar story with her, would Essie have found the friend's story shameful? Of course not! She would only have felt compassion for her friend and admiration for how she had come through such difficulty unbroken.

Could she extend that same kindness to herself?

Yes, she could. And she did. She realized clearly that it's the abuser, not the abused, who should more appropriately carry the burden of shame for their actions. She felt a shift in her self-esteem, which had been hurting for years. She knew who she was and that she was capable and strong. And this knowledge fed her new marriage. We can only show up fully for others when we show up fully for ourselves.

Rather than shun that period in her life and try to "stop thinking about it," which is where Essie was when we started, she has now integrated what happened into the fabric of her interesting life, and understands that the story contributes to the richness of who she is today, unfortunate as it was. So, windows open, floor well-vacuumed, the once-locked room in her house is now fully integrated into the whole framework of her life.

Challenge

Can we step aside from the tape that continuously plays in a loop inside our head and challenge ourselves to see things differently, from another perspective and make a kinder, gentler version of our stories... where we are the hero? Where despite life throwing us many curve balls, we learned, we grew, we survived and emerged victorious? And that would actually be a correct interpretation: life challenged us, we did our best, and survived. Possibly even thrived.

What a boost to our immune system that would be, not to mention our self-esteem and self-confidence!

Chapter 6

Co-Creation

The good news is, we are not in it alone... relax, surrender the illusion of control and ask for help.

Kathy, 34, had been a patient for a few years. I treated her using homeopathy for various ailments that she had over that time period. When she became pregnant with her second child, she experienced some nausea and tiredness in the first trimester, but did well with homeopathic remedies. As she approached her third trimester, however, her anxiety about the upcoming birth got worse and worse. The delivery of her first child had been extremely stressful. In fact, it had been an enormous disappointment. The baby had been in a good position, but had turned breech in the last few days before she was due and Kathy was forced to have a C-section. This was devastating to her as she had a natural birth all planned out in her mind. The recovery from the surgery was very tough, emotionally and physically.

Letting Go of Control

A few months after that birth, her daughter was diagnosed with asthma, and Kathy was sure it was due to having had a C-section, after reading an article saying that babies born by C-section had higher rates of asthma during their lives. She put herself under enormous pressure to have a vaginal delivery with this second baby. She ate very well, she exercised, she tried to sleep 7–8 hours a night and drink eight glasses of water per day. She tried to let go of stress by thinking positive thoughts. But in my office all she could do was cry. "I did everything right last time too, and still ended up with a C-section, I don't know what more to do!"

So much pressure, so much need to control. It's fine to have our preferences, it's fine (and necessary) to do everything in our power to have things unfold the way we want them to. And then, simply, we must *let go*. I explained to Kathy that her life and experiences are a co-creation. In fact, in this situation, there were three parties involved who had a say in how this birth would turn out: her, the baby and the Universe. To think that it was all on her shoulders to control an outcome that she had only a minority role in influencing was way too much pressure.

We can desire a natural birth with all our heart. We can do what is in our power to stack the odds in our favor. And then we have to recognize that we are not alone: there is something far greater than us that has a hand in the outcome. And the ability to recognize this adds a whole new perspective to the situation. We realize there is only so much *we* alone can do. So, an invitation is there to relax into the process – and even have some curiosity about how each situation in our life will unfold. We acknowledge that we are in partnership, in partnership with life.

In this case, Kathy was part of an orchestra of three, with each part of the ensemble essential to the outcome. Could Kathy relax and just do *her* third?

With this shift in perspective, she regained her emotional poise. She let go of her iron grip on the situation, a shift that, we agreed, could only help her move closer to achieving her goal.

I appreciate the word co-creation because it respects the concept of free will, and it acknowledges that there is some "higher involvement" in what happens. But more than this, I love the idea that, as in any partnership, we can ask for help. We can sometimes let the other lead. We don't need to know everything. And as in any good partnership, our partner is on our team, working for our higher good which will lead to some outcomes that are exactly the way we want them to be, and others that are not exactly what we hoped for.

And that's when we can feel that *it's all good*. When things happen not of our choosing or desire – maybe it's for the best anyway. Maybe the learning that we get when we go through the tougher stuff of life opens us up to growth that we would never choose, but that we greatly benefit from. And if we can see it that way, then it *is* all good.

As Kathy neared her due date, the baby seemed quite big. He was well-positioned but as with any vaginal birth after Caesarian (VBAC), the doctors get nervous if they feel that there are any factors which might put undue stress on the uterine scar tissue from the first birth. In this case, the size of the baby was becoming a risk factor. Kathy was under pressure to schedule a C-section date as she got closer to 40 weeks. The doctors pressured her into agreeing to a date at 39.5 weeks, saying that if she went into labor before that they would see how things progressed before rushing her into an emergency C-section.

Kathy was very upset. Cowed by fear, she agreed to a C-section date she felt was too early. She wanted to give her baby every chance to come naturally and at least give him until the actual due date to do so!

With my support, she called the hospital and postponed the surgery until her due date, at exactly 40 weeks. And, miraculously, she went into labor the day before the scheduled C-section! She delivered a beautiful and healthy baby boy vaginally and was exceptionally grateful to have had the experience. She learned firsthand that sometimes letting go of the outcome, while still advocating for yourself, can produce the desired results.

Being in co-creation doesn't mean you sit back with a shrug and say, "Well that's not what I want but I guess that's the way it is!" It means you do everything in your power to get things to be the way you want them to be, and then you let go and accept that what is must be for the best!

The best book I have read on this subject is *The Universe Has Your Back*, by Gabrielle Bernstein. We are here in co-creation with the Universe and if we are just able to recognize that fact, it can change everything.

Being Open to Co-Creation

Marie was in her forties and came to see me with major anxiety about work. She was a creative developer in an office that made software for famous video games. Prior to this job, she had spent her career working freelance on projects both big and small, and had been able to earn a fairly good living. Although she didn't relish working in a big office with all the politics, the steady salary and benefits were irresistible.

Her anxiety came up around producing creative work on demand, nine-to-five. She worked amongst very talented people and felt that her creative work was under constant scrutiny. She believed she was a very creative person, but her creativity flowed best when she had the space and time to ponder ideas, not when working a day job in a cubicle. She felt she was under the gun to *be creative now*. The pressure and the weight of the demands felt too much, and her resulting anxiety worked against her creative abilities.

Marie and I talked about creativity and inspiration. We talked about the idea of "co-creation": that her creativity rested not just on her shoulders, but was a result of a connection with something bigger than herself, whether we wanted to call that her guides, the Universe or Divine Energy. The fact is, Marie was working in conjunction with a creative force that was the inspiration and intuition she counted on daily to produce her work. She had just never named it as such.

Once she saw this force as something working with her but not exactly *her*, she felt an enormous sense of relief. She was not alone. Her work *was* a co-creation. She had help. She had always had this help, but now seeing it as such felt like a shared effort, a partnership. She made a conscious effort to connect with this energy in order to get into a creative flow by opening up to it and sensing where she needed to go next with her work.

This shift in perception had the effect of freeing her up and her anxiety lifted. The result was a huge breakthrough in creativity, which resulted in an invitation to present some work that she was doing in a writing class to a top producer at Netflix.

Trusting the Universe

An old patient, Cherry, made an appointment to see me after many years' absence. She was now 23 and I had treated her throughout her childhood primarily for acute illnesses, as her mother was a great believer in homeopathy and natural medicine. Now Cherry was studying for her MCAT exam to get into medical school. The exam was still four weeks away, but she was a bundle of nerves. She would study a section of the material, do a practice exam, grade it and compare it with her score on the last practice exams. Her mock exam scores were not consistently improving and she was panicking that she would not do well enough on her exam to get into the medical school of her choice. The more she recognized the possibility of failure, the more she froze.

We talked about why she wanted to go to medical school in the first place. She told me she had a great desire to help people heal who were struggling with neurological disease. Her own grandfather had died an ugly death from Parkinson's disease and her grandmother was suffering from Alzheimer's. She was determined to use her brains and talent to make a difference in this world: to try to alleviate the suffering of elderly people who had diseases for which there was currently no cure.

As she spoke about her desires and ambition, her whole face lit up. I could see her passion. Many young people who go to medical school go simply because they are smart enough to get in, some because their parents want them to, and some because they see it as a ticket to financial prosperity. But for Cherry, it was born of a passion and desire to make a difference. It was beautiful to see her speak about it.

I asked her what would happen if she didn't get into one of the top schools on her list. She started to cry and talked about all the people she would be letting down: the people who had coached her and supported her, the doctors who had given their time to have her on a rotation with them so she could see firsthand what it was all about, the doctors in a lab she worked in over the summer during an internship who were all rooting for her.

The thought of failing the exam and disappointing everyone was putting too much pressure on her. She felt she was giving it her best and wasn't able to do much better – but her thoughts were paralyzing her.

We talked through whether she would *really* be disappointing people, or was it truer that she would actually be disappointing herself. But more importantly, we were able to step back and realize together something that was very obvious to me: Cherry had a passion, and there is very little that can get in the way of that – because passion and desire are a calling out to the forces that be, a signaling to the Universe. Passion, like love, is very persistent. And it has the ability to attract forces of change to itself.

I encouraged her to be open enough to trust that she was in partnership with the Universe in her desire to create a life of professional service. And that it was not solely on her back. Yes, of course she had to study and do her best, but that she could do so with the confidence and knowledge that she was not doing it all alone, which lessened the pressure she had been feeling. She had help. Her passion, her desire and her yearning would call the Universe into partnership. The way forward would be hers to create and the Universe's to support.

It's true the outcome might not be the way she imagined it. She might get into a different school than her "top three," and her path may take an unanticipated turn. But it is, after all, a co-creation. To trust that she was not alone, that she had support, made the whole process of studying easier. A huge weight had been lifted and she knew her task was simply this: study, focus, do her best and trust that all would be well.

Passion is an unstoppable force; it can move mountains with its tenacity and ability to overcome obstacles.

Once we recognize that we are in partnership – whether it is in writing a script for a TV series, raising our children, taking an important exam, or going through an illness – the burdens become much lighter. When we acknowledge that we are loved and helped and that we are co-creating our reality, we can risk giving up some control and allow life to flow. It all works much better when we invite help and ask for guidance. This makes sense, for if the help and guidance were just imposed upon us, we would lose free will.

Humans have free will and the choice of how to steer their lives. Help comes when we are open to it, when we tap into our inner knowing, when we look for guidance and are available to receive it.

Challenge

Try it next time you are struggling: ask for help. Feel and connect with your spirit and open to any guidance. This guidance can come from our deep intuition, our spirit guides, the Universe, even from loved ones who have passed on and are often eager to help us!

This connection yields a greater result than whatever we can achieve alone.

Chapter 7

Gifts

*We receive a steady flow of "gifts" from the Universe to learn what we have come here to learn... if we don't like the suffering, **learn faster!***

Another patient I'll call Sally, managed to get herself out of a very bad marriage. When they first started dating, Joe was charming and wealthy, a brilliant man who was interested in many of the same things that Sally was: planetary health, architecture, esoteric matters. They married and started a family.

After a year or two, Sally started to notice some odd behaviors. Joe was frequently in litigation with various parties in his business dealings. He was often short of cash, and started borrowing money from her, twice using her credit card without permission and spending large sums of her money. Sally managed to rationalize this behavior, preferring not to see that which she didn't want to see. Most important to her was to feel safe and protected by her man, that he be strong and financially able to provide well for her and the kids.

The Perfect Gift

Things slowly unraveled when the IRS knocked on her door one day in search of her husband who they said was wanted for fraud. After the initial shock wore off, Sally began to look a bit more deeply into other financial matters and realized that her husband was a dishonest person who was conducting shady business dealings funded, in part, by her savings. How could she not have seen this? Had her need to feel protected blinded her to what was now completely obvious? On further investigation, she confirmed that he had stolen a large sum of money from her.

When confronted, he had a "plausible" reason and said he was planning to pay it all back.

Sally was forced to see that she had been hugely deceived by the person she had trusted the most – *herself!* She had let herself down by not seeing what she didn't want to see. It didn't take too long for her to realize that the neediness she felt in relationships came from her relationship with her dad – someone who was unreliable, unexpressive and with whom she had never felt safe or protected. Desperate to feel loved and cared for, she wanted it at any cost. And she paid a huge price, literally!

What's most amazing to me in this story is that Sally is a brilliant, beautiful and successful person in her own right. She owns her own business that has grown year by year. She came into the marriage at 35 years old, already quite wealthy herself from good investments she had made earlier in her life. She didn't really need a man to make her feel financially safe and cared for.

As painful as the ending of her marriage was, it was a huge opportunity for her to learn something very valuable.

She realized that she needed to make a shift: to *want* to be with a man, but not to *need* to be with one. She needed to deeply believe that she was strong and self-sufficient and capable on her own.

In a way that was hard to see at first, the ending of her marriage was a gift. A gift given by the Universe for her to learn and grow, and realize that a relationship based on neediness blinds us to reality.

I've come to see that the Universe always gives us the perfect gift! Like a partner who has known us forever, knows our exact clothing size, our favorite colors, the cuts that look good on us, our favorite fragrance, the Universe will make the gift to order. It will hurt us just as much as it needs to in order to get our attention, but no more. And if we can pull our head out of the sand for a few moments, we will see that the Universe's attention to detail is exquisite, everything perfectly orchestrated.

Of course, it is always our choice as to whether we want to accept the gifts of learning, or not. But the Universe is patient and will not be deterred – it will knock again next time if we refuse it. We are here to learn, and it's not always a picnic.

Sally went through a horrible divorce. Shortly after, she found herself attracted to an extremely wealthy and powerful man. He was married, but they started an affair. She told herself that it was perfect, after all she had gone through, she wasn't quite ready to get really involved with anyone again; a little fling on the side was just what she needed.

Little by little, however, she fell in love with him – but of course he was unavailable for much more than a few weekly meetings. How much would she put up with this time to have her needs for safety and security met?

The Universe keeps sending us "gifts" until we don't need them anymore. A big gift comes our way, and we are "broken open." We suffer enormously, we dig deep to cope, and we learn many things about ourselves. We vow to go forward, better. Then the Universe sends another gift our way, to see how serious we were about integrating the learning. Did we *really* get it? If we did, those gifts stop coming (I have no doubt we move on to another set of gifts, of course). If not, we will keep getting "re-gifted" again and again until we truly get it. My advice: if you don't like the gifts, learn the material.

How to learn the material? Own your part, see where you have responsibility for the problem and make the necessary changes in yourself so you can create a better pattern in your future.

Sally and I worked on creating new beliefs – "I am strong and independent and have everything I need to manage on my own," "I am my own best friend," "I take care of myself," "I trust myself and my judgment," "I have infinite value and worth."

Believing in herself would take away her need to be tucked

under someone's wing. This would hopefully ensure that when attracted to the next man, she will be acting out of genuine interest and not from fear and neediness.

Learning the Lesson

Carol, 40, had a somewhat related story. She was in her late thirties, relatively happily married with two kids. One day out of the blue her husband of six years told her he was leaving her. She was shocked and crushed. She asked if there was someone else but he said no. He was just no longer happy and wanted to be free.

She had done everything possible to go along with what he had needed, to not be a "bitchy" wife, to give him the space and freedom he seemed to always want – nights out with the boys, etc. – despite the fact that there were two young children at home and they both worked full time jobs. She could see in hindsight that she gave and gave in order to be loved and that maybe she had always sensed he wasn't quite happy. In a kind of desperation, she gave as much as possible with the kids and the household chores to make life easier for him.

In our work together, we were able to determine that Carol learned early on in her house growing up that being a good girl, and doing what everyone wanted, got her love and praise. It was very conditional. She became the ultimate pleaser. As a therapist I know once said, "Pleasers are the angriest people in the world." We worked to change her limiting beliefs about her own worth. From the place of knowing who she is and loving and valuing herself, changing patterns, habits and negative self-talk became easier.

Carol realized that she had not been very happy in the marriage either. She could admit that her husband was a selfish person who was acutely aware of his own needs, but not her needs or those of their young kids. It was very stressful to continuously have to try to buy her husband's love through her deeds and her generosity, which is what she had been subconsciously doing all along. She had much better clarity after the divorce, but it was very painful to see it.

Then came another gift. Carol met someone who was strong and domineering. He was very sure of himself and quite intense and they got quickly into a deep relationship. Her boyfriend was very controlling and had clear ideas about how things should be, how a woman should act, what he needed and wanted in the relationship. The sense of love and intensity between them fulfilled her deeply. She found herself bending her will to go along with things as he wanted them. The allure of his love was so fulfilling to her that she fell into the trap again.

Is it just a coincidence that this happened? Of course not! We attract the people who will reinforce the lessons we need to learn, and learn and re-learn if necessary. Compliments of the Universe. The trick is to see it sooner, understand the pattern faster, and make changes quicker.

It took a year (which was better than the six it took in her marriage) for Carol to see things clearly and break up the relationship once and for all. The misery of pleasing him to get his love, almost regardless of the demand, was a pattern she saw quickly – but it took every bit of strength she had to break it.

Finally free, after a great struggle, she met another man a few months later, whom she found very attractive. The only problem was, he was a bit aloof and non-committal. He had just gotten out of a long relationship himself and wasn't sure what he wanted. Ahhhh… again, the perfect gift! The perfect setup for her to give and give to see if she could win his love. And she tried. She dropped off freshly baked muffins in front of his door one morning to surprise him. She let him off the hook easily when he canceled plans at the last minute. Over-giving and over-understanding to get him to appreciate her, to see how good she was, to love her.

But she recognized the pattern quickly now. And she ended

it swiftly. She's decided that she wants to be Queen and if a man isn't interested in pleasing her, she's simply not interested in him.

I have no doubt her will on this will be tested again and again until she gets really good at loving herself, valuing herself and choosing well for herself. The Universe will continue to send her gifts in the form of various men or unappreciative bosses until it is no longer needed. But I can proudly tell you, she is learning fast and furiously!

It's not awful if we keep falling into the same trap – don't despair – it's the recovery time that matters! As long as we are getting better and better at recognizing and stopping the patterns we fall into, we are present in our lives and committed to creating a better outcome. It's beautiful to witness the progress.

Closed Down

One of my neighbors many years ago was a woman named Jill. Jill came from a large family and was one of the youngest. It was a busy family and Jill had learned to be very self-sufficient as a young girl as there wasn't much parental involvement in her life. Her dad was busy and her mom was a critical and demanding person.

Jill and her husband, Tom, had been trying to conceive for three years. It was a hard time, and her husband finally left, saying he didn't feel as though she loved him. Jill was shattered by his departure, because in fact, she had really loved Tom. But she pulled herself up by her bootstraps and made the best of things and soon remarried. Happily, the marriage was off to a good start and she was able to get pregnant soon after.

Over time, however, the marriage began to have similar difficulties as the first, with her new husband, Carl, wanting more of an emotional connection with her. Jill was very closed emotionally and analytical about everything, and found it difficult to express her feelings. This was unsatisfactory to Carl who often expressed his desire to feel closer to her.

Over time, Jill's parents died and left her a large sum of money. Smart as she was, Jill invested it in a risky venture and within a few months, in an unlucky turn of events, lost everything. This was devastating for Jill who had big plans for the money, which included buying land and building a vacation home for their family. The loss of this dream, and the loss of the money her father had worked so hard for was a devastating blow... one that might have had the ability to crack open even the most shut down person. But Jill showed no emotion about it. Carl tried to connect with her about the loss, but she wouldn't go there.

Time went on. Jill had a huge accident a short time later that by all rights should have cost her her life. She was hit by a truck while jogging one evening, but the truck never stopped. It was late in the evening and the intersection was deserted. Somehow, half-conscious, she managed to drag herself to a nearby house before collapsing. She was taken by ambulance to the hospital where she was found to have a severe concussion and a number of broken bones. The doctor at the hospital commented that she was lucky to have survived the accident.

Carl saw this as a second chance for them – how lucky she was still alive! How blessed and grateful they should be for a second chance! Jill had no similar epiphany and no ability to connect with her husband in processing the accident with him emotionally – another missed opportunity.

Carl was beyond frustrated – without the emotional connection, intimacy on all levels had suffered. He didn't know what to do – he loved Jill but didn't feel close to her. He didn't want to leave, mostly because of the kids.

Knock knock knock – is anybody home? What will it take? What more had to happen to her, to them, for Jill to connect to herself, and to Carl? A spiritual person, he saw Jill as having come here to learn how to feel, how to reconnect with her heart. Life was giving her plenty of invitations to learn this, but she was impervious to all of them, still continuing to process everything solely with her reasoning, rational mind.

Time passed. At age six, their youngest child, Amy, was diagnosed with a brain tumor and underwent numerous surgeries with chemo and radiation for over a year. And that little girl suffered greatly. Carl was beside himself; he couldn't bear to watch his daughter in such distress, uncertain whether she would live or die. Jill went through the event strong and resolute, apparently without shedding a tear, at least to Carl's knowledge. Rather than Amy's ordeal making them closer, holding and comforting each other, they went through it separately: he with his friends and family and Jill, alone. When asked by others how she was doing, she would reply, "Me? I'm okay, it's Amy who is suffering so much." Carl couldn't bear to see that Amy's suffering didn't seem to result in any personal suffering for Jill, but at best, merely sympathy for their daughter. It was hard to take.

Miraculously, Amy recovered. But what would it take for Jill? Why the resistance to feeling and expressing? How much suffering does a person have to invite – unconsciously, for sure – in order to learn and grow?

Carl pushed to begin couple's therapy, which they did. Carl made it clear to Jill that he would leave if he was unable to feel closer to her. He accepted that Jill was an emotionally unexpressive person, but for him emotional closeness was a pre-requisite for a happy marriage.

Challenge

The Universe is very creative and unrelenting in helping us fulfill our life's goals here on Earth. I don't mean our material or professional goals, I mean our spiritual goals. It will keep sending gifts our way until the lessons are completed; they've got an endless supply of wrapping paper up there it seems.

In every situation that challenges us, what would it take

for us to look deeply inside and ask ourselves, with genuine curiosity… what's in this situation for me to learn, about myself, about life? Why am I confronted with this? What do I need to see and learn from this problem; how can I grow? Why was I gifted with this?

Maybe if we were trained at an early age to consider life's challenges from this point of view, we would evolve more painlessly, rather than having to live similar difficulties over and over again. It's worth considering.

What would it feel like to see some of the difficulties in your life as gifts, opportunities to learn and evolve, and accumulate wisdom? Realizing that the sooner you "get it," the sooner the pain diminishes…

Chapter 8

Regret

Idealizing the road not taken is a recipe for misery...

Regret is one of the most frustrating of all emotions. Here's why: when we regret and look back on the path not taken with longing, wistfully thinking that we should have chosen it after all, because the choice we made did not work out well, as well as the other choice would have – we do ourselves a grave disservice.

The funny thing about this method of self-torture, is that we *assume* that the path we didn't choose would have worked out in the most ideal way. And that's ridiculous! We have no idea how the other paths not chosen would have worked out at all, and as such, how absolutely cruel to torture ourselves with what could have been... when the idealized outcome of any other option is pure fantasy.

Mathematically speaking, in terms of our satisfaction with the outcome, the path we did not choose would have worked out either better, the same, or worse than the path we did choose, right? We have a 66% chance of the road not taken leading to either a worse or similar satisfaction level as the path we did choose! Why make up a story that if only we had chosen another path, it all would have been great? There is absolutely no evidence of that!

If you see my point of view here, you can vow to never, ever have regrets again. You can tell yourself you made the best decision possible in the moment, with what you knew at the time. There might be untold treasures in the path you did choose that have yet to make themselves known. Trust yourself, trust the Universe.

Desperate to Have a Child

Another patient of mine, Alice, got married in her mid-thirties. She was eager to have children and though her husband, Pete, had reservations about it, he was willing to go along. After months of trying: no pregnancy. They each had medical exams, and the doctors determined that they both had physical issues preventing a possible pregnancy. Pete had a varicocele which was operable and would likely solve the problem on his part, but for Alice it was graver: she had premature ovarian failure which meant that, even though she was still relatively young, her eggs were no longer able to be fertilized.

She was desperate to have a child and the only option, besides adoption, was finding an egg donor: someone who would donate an egg, which would be fertilized with her husband's sperm, and implanted in her. It involved her taking large doses of hormones.

Pete flat-out refused. He said he wasn't sure he wanted kids in any case, and to have a child that was not genetically hers was of no interest to him. He was also concerned about her health and the effect of all those hormones in the long run. Alice was crushed, but since Pete had been on the fence all along, she decided to respect his wishes and not coerce him into it.

Time passed. Most of her friends had kids, and those kids passed through childhood and adolescence while she looked on. She had a deep sadness about the situation, with Mother's Day every year the ultimate insult, as if to further rub her face in her loss. She started to regret deeply that she had not pursued having a baby even if it meant forcing the issue with her husband. She became angry and resentful toward him. Maybe she should have even left him to have a child on her own?

Every time she saw a pregnant woman she burned with envy. Every time she saw a cute baby in a carriage she knew that it might have been hers. Of course, what she regretted not pursuing was the best case scenario – that she would have found an egg donor, that the egg would have been quickly fertilized, that she would have carried the baby to term, that the baby would have been born healthy, that her husband would have been just as thrilled with the new arrival as she was and stayed with the marriage during the trials and tribulations of a newborn, that she would have tolerated the hormones she would have needed to take and that they wouldn't have caused her to have cancer in later years, etc. That's a lot of ifs!

Do you see where I am going with this? We cannot regret! Because in doing so, we make up a fantasy in our heads that what *might* have been *would* have been and we have no way of knowing that – the chances of the other paths working out in the best-case scenario are not at all a given!

What Alice really needed to do was grieve. That would have been of great benefit in coming to terms with the loss of the possibility, the closing of that door, to have a child. Sure, she cried here and there about it, but I don't believe she ever truly grieved it. What an opportunity to go down into the swamp of her darkest feelings and yell, cry and rage out all of her disappointments and frustrations.

When we take the time to let our darkest feelings exist, and give ourselves permission to feel them, we allow ourselves to heal. We can express them in the company of a friend or a therapist, or alone if we feel safe enough. Sometimes music can better allow the powerful emotions to flow through us. 5Rhythms dance is an effective tool for processing deeply held emotions, such as grief, as it encourages us to release them through movement.

And this, in fact, is most likely where we need to go with regret, which is grieving the disappointment of the outcomes of our choices: the pain of not getting what we wanted – *not* in longing for a future that likely wouldn't have happened anyway had we chosen differently.

The Danger of "What If"

I know a woman, Laura, who had deep regret about certain values she felt she had failed to raise her children with. She herself had grown up in a family of three children. Each of them had grown up and moved away from home for marriages and job opportunities. As adults they lived thousands of miles away from each other. They tried to see each other yearly, and were in somewhat regular contact, but the physical distance made it hard for them all to feel close.

Laura's husband, on the other hand, had grown up in a family of six brothers and sisters, all of whom stayed in the city in which they were raised, living in relatively close proximity to each other. But her husband was busy and traveled a lot, so was not particularly close with any of his siblings.

The couple had three children, all teenagers when I met Laura. Her daughter, who was the oldest, had left home to attend school in another state. She was not close with her brothers. The brothers fought constantly and were very different from each other. In fact, none of the three kids were close.

Whenever Laura spent time in the company of other families and saw the kids in those families getting along, enjoying each other's company, going out on weekends to attend events and parties together, she would feel extremely sad. She saw that she had failed to raise her kids with the value of the importance of family, the importance of seeing their brothers and sisters as being unique and irreplaceable. She should have encouraged them – if not insisted – throughout their childhood that they always be close and be there for one another.

Upon reflection, Laura realized that one of her own values had been to grow up free and independent, not tied down to any particular place. She consciously raised her kids to feel that they could live anywhere and do anything they wanted – that the world was a wide-open place, full of opportunities. She didn't quite realize that it was a very different message than the importance of family and being close with family.

She came to realize that her message to them might encourage them to become adults who would have weak ties to each other. She herself had been raised with a "the world is wide open for you" message and had actually thrived on that: she had lived in numerous countries and had several different careers. But only from the point of view of a parent did she realize that she might suffer, as her parents probably had, as a result of her kids putting their own goals and desires ahead of family ties.

She realized she would likely suffer from the lack of closeness that she might ultimately have with her children, and they might have with each other, if they elected to all go their separate ways and live apart from each other. She regretted not having stressed to them the value of family and putting family relationships as a priority.

What deep regret! It seemed far too late now to go back and try to send that message; no one was open to hearing it. She continued to have a deep pain in her heart when she heard how kids in other families enjoyed being with each other and got along so well. Her family seemed so broken and dysfunctional, particularly in the dynamic between the kids.

How to live with this, with the pain and perpetual sadness of wishing we had done things differently? One answer is to realize that maybe the story we create in our minds isn't actually true. In this particular instance, Laura's thought that "If only I had instilled those family values when they were young, my kids would be close to each other now and feel a commitment to staying close" is not necessarily true. There's no way she could know what might have been different if she had taught her kids differently. The kids might very well have grown up exactly the same.

In reality, the non-verbal messages the kids were getting from viewing their parents' lives was the same one as the verbal message they got: their mom lived very far from her siblings and as a result wasn't especially close to them, and in fact was closer to the friends she had made over the years. Their dad was not a man who valued close relationships, preferring to put his time and energy into his hobbies and interests.

So, how effective would that verbal message have been for the kids, even if she had given it diligently, given that the words and pictures didn't match? In other words, what the kids actually *saw* were two parents who had not put family first in their own choices, so how effective would different words have been?

Seeing it this way, Laura realized that she probably had limited ability to instill this message to begin with. "Do what I say, not what I do" is a maxim that is often ineffective in raising kids. And this is not even to mention the role that genetics and epigenetics possibly had on her kids' temperaments. Is it possible that having a sense of independence and self-sufficiency are genetic characteristics that had been passed on by both parents? Would any verbal teaching that Laura had given been able to overcome her children's possible pre-dispositions? Unlikely.

So, while the outcome was still sad for Laura: that her family was not close and moreover didn't seem to value closeness as she would have liked, she could now see that she may not have been able to have that influence on her kids even if she had parented differently. She saw that she needed to stop torturing herself with regret about what she could or should have done or said differently in raising them. There was no evidence at all that doing anything differently would have led to the outcome she wanted and to keep telling herself that it would have was a lie that resulted in great suffering.

We never know where the "If only..." path leads, so why regret that we didn't take it?

Healing through Self-Reflection

I always find it very touching and humbling when someone is able to see circumstances from a place of deep inquiry and curiosity rather than from defensiveness and blaming. Over a Sunday morning coffee, a long-time friend, Michelle, confided in me that she had deep regrets about how she had conducted herself in her marriage.

After her 25-year marriage ended a few years ago, Michelle was enraged. It's true that she had not been happy for many years in the marriage; she often had nothing positive to say about her husband or their relationship. But she had been willing to hang in there. She valued her commitment and maintaining the family structure for her three teenage children, and wouldn't have compromised that by leaving.

In a deeply shocking move though, her husband one day announced *he* was leaving. Michelle couldn't believe it. She had been willing to sacrifice her happiness "for the greater good," but he was not? After lawyers and difficult negotiations about money and kids, Michelle was left with a much lower standard of living – and so were the kids. She had just started a new business that was not yet financially viable and many of the luxuries that the children were used to were now unaffordable – private schools, summer camps, vacations, etc. – as her ex-husband was no longer willing to shoulder the burden of them. She truly hated him and didn't go to great lengths to hide that from the kids.

This story is fairly common. But what was uncommon was Michelle's ability to look deeply within herself and come to an honest appraisal, though it certainly took a number of years to get there.

She confided in me that she realized that she wasn't very happy with who she had been as a wife. She realized that she hadn't been a good communicator about her needs and concerns and had stored deep resentments and anger toward her husband during their years together. She frequently "punished" him by withdrawing physically and emotionally. She had been extremely critical of him and her dislike was readily apparent.

She hadn't found him to be a good husband nor an involved parent and had made no bones about it.

In her self-reflection and realizations, she became very sad and regretful. What if she had been able to play her part better? What if she had been able to resolve her differences with him more constructively? Had she just taken on the role of her critical mother whose marriage had also ended in divorce when Michelle was young?

Maybe theirs wouldn't have been the ideal marriage, but they would still have had a united family. The kids would have had one home to come back to on their college breaks and to celebrate holidays. Financially they would not have paid such a big price, not to mention how the kids had suffered and changed as a result of the ugly divorce and continued poor relationship between their parents. The regret was tormenting. If only she had realized what she had, instead of focusing on what was missing, they would all be better off today.

It was heartbreaking to hear her express this pain. It was also hard to say, "There, there don't feel that way, it might not have been very good for anyone had you stayed. The home environment was toxic as it was." Who knows what would have happened had she had this self-awareness then and the marriage had survived? But one thing was very clear to me: that as a result of the divorce, Michelle had gleaned some deep insights which had led to a new understanding of herself. The very process of self-reflection that came out of the suffering had enabled her to deeply see herself and understand some important truths. Well, maybe that was the whole point. Would she have been able to learn all of that had the marriage continued? Highly unlikely.

Sometimes things do seem "regrettable," but all was not for nothing. I can't speak for the other members of the family, but Michelle's insights helped her evolve personally to a great degree. Isn't that what it's all about? Of course, it would be preferable if this type of knowledge could be acquired more gracefully, and I believe life often gives us a chance to do so, but at a certain point the timer goes off and it's time to get the lessons in, one way or the other.

We can only do our best with what we know in the moment. Looking backwards from a point of greater wisdom and regretting that we didn't have the clarity then that we have now is very unkind to ourselves, especially when we berate ourselves for it.

Very Bad Luck

There is one story that has haunted me since I heard it. A lovely woman named Grace and her husband, Fred, had been married for about 10 years. It was a second marriage for both of them. She had been in her late sixties and he in his early seventies one day when he fell off a ladder trying to repair something on the roof of their house.

Although he was in excellent health, she had begged him many times not to climb to the roof, but to hire someone to do these types of repairs instead. It had been a winter day with snow on the ground and she had been out running some errands. Fred had climbed the ladder to get onto the roof, lost his balance and fell to the ground. Miraculously a neighbor heard him calling for help and he was rushed to the hospital in an ambulance. He had broken his neck and irreparably injured his spinal cord resulting in permanent paralysis from the neck down.

One year later, he survives on pain meds 24/7 in a long-term care facility. Life as he knew it was forever changed, as was their life together. They had to cancel many plans and dreams and sell their house to pay for the medical costs. Such grief and heartbreak!

How is she not furious with him for his poor judgment? How can he live not regretting his decision to go up the ladder that morning? It seems it would require super-human abilities not to have regrets in this case.

Regrets are pointless, they change nothing, just add insult to injury. Even as I relay this story, a small voice in my head still whispers, "but what do you know anyway about their paths, what they needed to learn individually and together, and how do you know that this is actually not the best place right now for each of them?" I don't. It takes an extraordinary amount of faith to go there, which feels like it stretches my own limits at times.

It's hard to say that what happened is not regrettable. There's no *obvious* good that came out of his fall. We can't tell ourselves that we are making up a story by imagining a better outcome if he had not gone up the ladder. We can make up almost any better outcome if he had not gone on the ladder that day – and likely be right! Sigh. At this point, we must go back to accept. Some things seem way bigger than is possible for us to understand. We must go to accept because it *is*.

Very often when it comes to regret, the need for forgiveness is the final piece in healing. Often there is simply a need to forgive ourselves. Sadly, we could not have known then what we now know. Forgive, forgive, forgive. Many of us hold ourselves to an impossibly high standard that we would never hold anyone else to!

If it's someone else that needs our forgiveness, we must deeply know that by not forgiving them, it's a grudge we hold within ourselves. And that grudge is a poison to us… the person who hurt us is left unaffected. So, it's a double whammy – we are hurt by what "they did" and we continue to hurt ourselves by keeping the anger alive with our grudge.

Changing our limiting beliefs can help us forgive. We can rewire our brains to believe that: "I can forgive, I have the ability to forgive, I desire to forgive, I know how to forgive. I release all grudges in my heart with ease and grace."

Challenge

Is there a fork in the road that you often look back on with regret?

A decision, a choice, a path you took which you've now labeled as bad, wrong or a mistake? "If only I hadn't…"

I encourage you to re-think this! Is it possible you're exactly where you need to be in your life, right now… a product of all the decisions you've made along the way? And that it would be impossible to pull one decision out of the mix, like pulling one thread out of the weave, and predict how things would be today if you had made different choices?

Be here, now. Ram Dass

Chapter 9

Death

Home at last... what a long, strange trip it's been!

Fear of Obliteration

A patient of mine, Paul, who is 62, came to see me with troubling anxiety. Essentially, his anxiety focused on his health. He was always very anxious about having his yearly blood tests, for fear the doctors would find something terrible. Not surprisingly, he had "white coat hypertension," high blood pressure when taken in the doctor's office, but not when he took it himself at a pharmacy. Every little ache or pain began a sequence of worrying about what it might be... possibly cancer? In actuality, his health was excellent, so his fears were not founded in any present reality. He was tired of living with this feeling of an ax hanging over his head, so he called me to work on it.

As we began to explore it, we quickly saw that it was not actually a fear of getting sick that he had, but a fear of death. Of course, illness, especially in the later part of life, often and eventually does lead to death. And he was acutely aware of that. So any sign of ill health was proof to him that death was around the corner. And that was terrifying to him.

What is so scary about death? It's true that in our culture we avoid the topic of death like the plague (no pun intended!). Even among those who are near death, it is uncomfortable to discuss. Adult children often feel uncomfortable to broach the subject with dying parents or terminally ill relatives. "Don't be negative," they are admonished! Negative? The person is dying, why is denial a better option? Wouldn't it be a relief to open it up as a topic: "So, mom, what do you think awaits you on the other side?" Often times, the dying person would like very much to talk about these things but is afraid to scare the others.

We are all doing to die. A good friend of mine likes to say, "None of us are getting out of this alive!" So, why is the topic so taboo? Because the unknown is scary!

In Paul's case, rather than work on the anxiety (the result of the problem), we set our sights a bit higher and worked on the cause of the problem – the fear of death. If the fear of death was there because death was scary, and death was scary because it was an unknown, how could we make the concept of death, and more specifically Paul's own death, a more comfortable topic?

Delving into Paul's childhood, it was easy to discover where the fear of death came from. On at least three occasions that he was able to recall, people close to him died when he was a young boy, the first being his grandfather with whom he was very close. On the morning of his grandfather's death, his parents simply announced to him, rather gruffly as he remembers it: "Your grandfather's dead. No crying!"

There was no discussion, no consolation, no explanation, no offering of the classic, "He's in a better place now," which while mysterious, seems to confer some solace. There was no open grieving and the family simply never mentioned his grandfather again. I'm sure Paul's parents were people who themselves had no idea how to cope with death or grief.

For Paul, death became a terrifying thing from that moment on – from one minute to the next you were here and then you were gone, disappearing as if you had never existed. All he could remember was seeing his grandfather's coffin being lowered into the ground – how awful! And it seemed taboo to mention the deceased as if, God forbid, it would induce sadness among the living!

Associating death with obliteration, *of course* Paul found death personally terrifying.

When I was in my twenties, I was convinced people throughout the ages had simply made up the concept of God as a crutch, to console themselves during life's difficulties and to feel better about what lay on the other side of death. My own spirituality has grown gradually over the past 30 years, fed by many books and numerous memorable visits to psychics and channelers.

In my early forties, after both my parents had passed on, I was introduced to a channeler and scheduled the first of numerous sessions with her. The conversations we had were nothing short of astonishing, as the channeler mentioned details and events about my life and my parents' lives with such accuracy as to leave **no doubt** in my mind that my parents were still "there," communicating through her.

Since then, I have a deep understanding that there is "life" after death, and that it is far more glorious than the one we live here. But I consider these very personal beliefs and ones that I am not in a position to attempt to convince my patients of.

Paul, of course, had no imaginings of what lay on the other side. The whole topic was taboo and he had never allowed himself to venture there in his mind. The people he knew who had died during his childhood all seemed to disappear suddenly, with no explanation, and there was no one around who wanted to answer his questions on the topic. The adults were too uncomfortable or sad to go there themselves.

I introduced Paul to Eben Alexander's books and documentary. Dr. Alexander is a neurosurgeon who contracted a fatal form of meningitis and went into a coma. Inexplicably, he made an absolutely impossible full recovery – and even more crazily – he came back with full memory of his time spent during the coma. In his very credible account, there is certainly an "afterlife." Interestingly, his NDE (Near Death Experience) was very similar to the many other accounts of what happens after the spirit leaves the body and crosses to the other side.

Anita Moorjani also wrote a very convincing book describing her encounter with the afterlife during an NDE. Both accounts have amazingly similar details of the unfathomable love and beauty awaiting us after death. Both people felt so liberated in "death," that when they realized they had to "return to their bodies" neither wanted to do so, despite having families and loved ones still here.

My deep familiarity with the literature on NDEs has left me with the conviction that the afterlife (or between-life, if you will) is a magical place filled with great love and beauty. Life on Earth is the illusion, despite the fact that many of us here think that this is all there is, that this is indeed the destination.

After Paul started becoming familiar with these accounts and the topic of death in general, the whole subject became less scary. In fact, it became fascinating. We worked to change his limiting beliefs about death – most notably that he would cease to exist in all forms and that he would be unsafe and alone.

We actually don't *know* firsthand (or maybe it's more correct to say we don't *remember* firsthand) about death, so why choose beliefs that make us scared and miserable? At a minimum, let's have beliefs that are open, neutral and interested in what the next chapter might bring (since it's inescapable anyway!).

Soon Paul became open to the wider possibilities of what happens after we die. Obliteration and loneliness were not part of the picture he began to form in his mind of death and after death. He read voraciously on the subject. At the same time, the anxiety about his health started to diminish. He could more comfortably say that he knew he was going to die someday and that he accepted that. He actually began to see the next chapter as something he was even curious about.

What he couldn't believe was how his close friends reacted when he tried to broach the subject with them and share his enthusiasm for all he had learned. They shut him down so fast he was shocked. It was where he himself had been only a few months earlier!

Anxiety about health is often rooted in fear of death. How funny that the one thing that is guaranteed to happen to each and every one of us is so terribly unsettling to most. For sure, people who have no spiritual or religious beliefs have much more difficulty around this topic. Those who believe that when we die we are buried six feet under in a wooden box *and that's that* are the ones who are more difficult to help shift their perspective. That scenario does sound lonely and scary. I'm not at all in favor of making up a story just to feel better. In my case, I am simply, totally convinced.

Michael Pollan in his book, *How to Change Your Mind*, talks about how psychedelics have been used in research among the terminally ill who exhibited anxiety about dying. During their psychedelic journeys, the research subjects invariably felt they had connected with "God" or a divine energy – a feeling of boundless love and beauty. This alone was enough to greatly diminish their anxiety around dying and they were able to more peacefully accept their imminent fate.

The NDE research by Raymond Moody spanning decades has brought forward the similarity in experiences among people who have "crossed over" to the other side and then, for whatever reason, come back to their bodies and regained consciousness. Most tell of not wanting to come back to their lives on Earth, of not wanting to leave the incredible love and peace they found during their mini-death. The vast majority of those lived their remaining years free of fear of death. The material is out there – familiarize yourself with it before rejecting it!

The soul lives on after death: it goes "back home." Details are uncertain, different religions promise different descriptions of what awaits. Deeply accepting that we continue on after death, in whatever form and in whatever way, diminishes our fear of death and thus, our anxiety about health.

Fear of Suffering

After treating Stuart for his year-round allergies, he casually mentioned to me that his anxiety was ruining his life. On the outside he had it all: a good marriage, three grown-up kids who were all doing very well, his own company which was hugely profitable, lots of free time during the day to pursue his interests.

He exercised rigorously five times a week, was extremely careful about his diet, saw the doctor yearly for appropriate check-ups and exams. He had a naturopath, a homeopath and a meditation coach who made up his "alternative" health team. He confided to me that while he seemed easy going and relaxed on the outside, he was haunted by anxiety about getting sick. In his case, he was simply terrified about the possibility of suffering.

At 57, he had been witness to a number of people who had died of cancer or protracted illnesses. While he wasn't thrilled with the idea of dying, and in fact had a lot of fear around it, the thought of being in pain was more than he could bear to think about. As a result, he did everything in his power to manage his health, and if he slipped up at all, on his diet in particular, he worried himself sick about it. Ironically, all the stress he created for himself in his attempts to have the perfect lifestyle was likely harmful enough to offset all the good he was doing!

Eckhart Tolle said it best in his book, *The Power of Now*: when we spend the present moment either regretting the past or worrying about the future, we actually miss our whole lives, which can only be lived in the present moment. The present moment is all we actually have! If we aren't present for it, but rather spend it in either the past (which is gone) or the future (that has not yet happened), we lose a precious opportunity.

It seemed to me this was at the heart of Stuart's problem. The present was lovely, but he was unable to enjoy it very much as it was mostly spent in a miserable future of imagined bodily suffering. If Stuart could simply remain present for the present, there would be no problem. We have no idea what the future holds for us. Maybe Stuart would die at a ripe old age in his sleep, with no suffering at all. What a shame to have wasted all these wonderful years worrying, when it wasn't going to happen anyway. It's not as if the worrying affords us some kind of protection!

We worked to rewire his subconscious beliefs to be able to trust himself to embrace and navigate whatever life had to offer, to be courageous facing the unknown, knowing that he had the skills and resources to always find the best solutions for himself, and to live his life fully invested in the present, letting the past go and allowing the future to take care of itself.

Terrified of Meds

While treating a colleague named Jerry a number of years ago, we also hit a wall of worry and anxiety about death. But in his case there was a different spin on it. A firm believer in naturopathy and homeopathy, he was committed to this path for his health and the health of his family members. But, at age 60, he suffered from idiopathic high cholesterol – meaning that the cause was likely genetic, not related to his lifestyle, which was impeccable.

Jerry was vegan and rarely if ever cheated. He worked out five days a week at a gym and enjoyed activities that kept him physically fit, such as regular tennis games with his son. He took all the right supplements. But year after year, he still had high cholesterol. He didn't want to die prematurely and was terrified. His family doctor, whom he saw reluctantly and only to get his yearly blood tests done, bullied him each year after the results came back, "You need to be on cholesterol-lowering drugs, you're playing with fire! At this rate, you'll have a stroke and live (or die) to regret it!" And each year, Jerry would leave the doctor's office, dejected, feeling like his body had failed him again.

He was terrified that he would eventually have to break down, go against his values, and go on those detested drugs in a medical system he despised, supporting the pharmaceutical companies he hated. How long would he be able to resist? His worry about whether he would have the courage to follow through on his values if his health got worse tormented him.

What scared him almost more that an untimely death, was being bullied into a treatment that he did not believe in.

Now, how about that present moment? Jerry's cholesterol had been stable year to year and he was not presently in any real danger. The doctor's admonishments were more about the future. Wouldn't it be better to believe that, should things get worse, he would not be sucked, helplessly, into the medical system as if by a vacuum, but would be able to do the proper research to find the best solutions for himself, given whatever treatments, natural or pharmaceutical, were available at the time?

I shared with Jerry a study I was familiar with that showed that patient outcomes were significantly affected by whether they believed in the treatments they were undergoing. Patients with cancer who believed that the chemotherapy would cure them and envisioned the medication entering their tumors and killing the cancer cells had increased survival rates versus patients who believed the chemo was poisoning them but that, regrettably, they had no other choice but to take it.

Jerry and I changed his limiting beliefs that he was doomed, that he was helpless in the face of the medical machine. We replaced old beliefs with beliefs that he was in control of his destiny, that he could trust himself to make the very best choices about his health, whatever they might be. That just like any business problem he was used to solving on a daily basis, he would collect the facts, look at the options and make the best possible choices.

We also worked on understanding that at the end of either road he chose – pharmaceutical or natural – lay death: that ultimately, he would die. Though natural medicine could prolong his life, it wouldn't, in fact, spare him from death. Seeing that the outcome of either choice would eventually be the same, and that there was no guarantee of additional timing on either path, freed him up from the pressure of making the "wrong" decision. It's not as if in picking the "correct" treatment he could forever cheat death; no, not at all.

Wow, what a shift in perspective for Jerry: a new trust in himself that he could navigate his own health without worrying that his fear of death would cause him to betray his values. And knowing that at the end of either path he chose, he faced the same result, amounted to much less pressure and anxiety.

Isn't it better to face the prospect of death with a certain calm and prepare mentally, emotionally and spiritually for it now?

Worrying Robs the Joy

On a monthly basis, I have new mothers joining my practice seeking treatment for their babies. Some are inquiring about alternatives to vaccines, some simply want help getting their babies over colic and sleeping better. Having a new baby is in many ways terrifying, to be sure. Suddenly, we are responsible for this small being whom we love as we have never known love before.

I get to know many of these moms through their child-bearing years and am often sad to see their anxiety increase with each new child, not decrease as one would expect as their experience and confidence grows. The responsibility feels overwhelming, with each cough and cold representing a potentially life-threatening illness. Sometimes the stress is so great that it seems there is very little joy at all for these women in motherhood.

This is not even to mention the effect that all the worrying has on the child. It's difficult for a child to grow up feeling strong and safe when his mom is always worrying about him. What kind of message does it send? Interestingly, many of these moms admit to being similar to their own mother, who worried continuously about them. This worry, often intertwined and confused with love, is not a gift to transmit to your child!

I've worked with many of these moms directly on this issue,

and have found that underlying all the stress is an enormous fear of death. What if... the unthinkable happens? We would be foolish if we did not acknowledge, that yes, death for any of us at any time *is* a possibility. We have all heard of someone who knows someone...

One of my dearest friends lost her son to cancer when he was 12. And then my own son danced with death numerous times during his illness. It is there, lurking as a possibility, 100% of the time. But how to make peace with this so anxiety does not rule our lives? Because if we don't do this, the joy of living is largely snuffed out. We become so worried and exhausted from worry that we miss out on much of the fun of raising our children.

The Illusion of Control

I occasionally reference my eventual death with my children so they understand to appreciate me, and everyone in their lives, because we will not always be here together. I have also shared my belief that my soul is simply inhabiting my body for the time being and will leave once the rental agreement has expired – but that surely we will be together again once we all arrive "back home."

Death is a part of life, obviously, but the way we actually live this fact is with terror. If we could know for certain that death was but a "momentary" separation, and that we would all meet again in due time... well, the pain of the temporary loss would still be there, but mitigated somewhat.

The Mexican festival Dia de Muertos, Day of the Dead, celebrates the dead with a clear understanding that the souls of their beloveds are just on the other side of the curtain. Their deep belief in the afterlife makes death a far less foreboding topic.

Becoming more comfortable with death is about accepting the journey and surrendering control, or I should say, the illusion of control. Death is a real fact for ourselves and those we love; it's not something that happens only to other people! Talking about it is not morbid. Keeping it hush hush is what creates the fear. Could we start to introduce the topic, and all the mystery that surrounds it... and bring it out of the closet and into our lives?

I cannot end this chapter, without talking a bit more about grief. Grief and death are obviously related, but I want to explore the concept of grieving, not solely associated with dying. Grief, like death, is another extremely difficult area for people to find the willingness to address.

Fear of Grieving

A patient that I have known for 20 years made an appointment to see me about a year after her mom died unexpectedly. Her mom was briefly sick and died quickly, leaving Sylvia very little time to get used to the idea that it was the end of her mom's life. The loss of her mom resulted in an enormous hole in her life; a crater, in fact. Sylvia had four kids under 10 at the time and a husband who was busy trying to provide for them all. Her mother had always been there for her, and was also her best friend.

I asked Sylvia how the grieving was going. She looked at me oddly. "Who has time to grieve?" she asked me. After the funeral, it was right back to business as usual, managing the kids, helping her husband in his business where she could, just trying to keep all the balls up in the air. The way she regarded the process of grieving was as if it was an indulgence, sort of like a vacation, or a visit to the spa. Who has time for that with all that's going on?

But looking a bit deeper at it, time wasn't really the issue. It was fear. Afraid to really feel the loss, she avoided it. Afraid that if she allowed herself to cry and miss her mom, she might never stop – and then what would happen to her and all her responsibilities? And even if she had the courage to "go there," where would she do it? Alone in her room? That seemed so sad and pathetic to her. How would she do it: simply start thinking about her mom until she got sad, and then cry? She wasn't even sure she could cry, she was now so accustomed to holding it all back. When should she do it? Tonight, tomorrow night, next weekend? When her husband was home so he could watch the kids? He had already pretty much told her to get over it, it had been a year already. Maybe put a date on the calendar for next week when she would be home alone in the house? It all felt so awkward.

For many of us, grieving feels anything but natural. In our culture of busyness and efficiency, many people are encouraged to skip the step of grieving, to simply push past and allow time itself to "heal all wounds," apparently letting us off the hook completely. And since grieving seems so awkward and unpleasant anyway, we're just as happy to do that.

And what about the other griefs in life, not as large as death maybe, but griefs about break-ups, about failures, about all the areas in life which didn't turn out as we thought they would, as we thought they should? Where's the time to grieve and move through those things? There is none. We are encouraged just to sweep past things and never process the disappointment or the hardship.

Working through Grief

Meditation can be a great help in these circumstances. Simply creating a space and time, sitting and following the breath, to be present to how we feel. If grief comes up we can see it, we can acknowledge it, we can feel it... and observe it as it moves and changes.

Stan Grof's Holotropic Breathwork is also an effective tool for moving though grief. It refers to a process in which deep, fast breathing, in a supported context such as a therapy session or retreat, brings us into a trance-like experience of going deeply inside ourselves. This state can be inherently healing, bringing to the surface any issues that need addressing and helping the practitioner resolve them in a meaningful way.

Mama Gena, author of the book *Pussy* and founder of the School of Womanly Arts, calls this process of deep grieving "Swamping": when we go down into the swamp and we yell it out and cry it out and rage out all our disappointments. During this process, she encourages us to move our bodies, ideally to music, to let the powerful emotions flow through us. This is a practice to help us process and release stuck emotions.

Sylvia and I talked about her finding the courage to cry about her mom, to truly feel her loss. Not only for herself, but as a model for her kids to see how to process the loss. She was sick and tired of feeling sick and tired and was willing to try. As well, I gave her a homeopathic remedy to help balance her emotions around the grief, which made things better over the ensuing weeks.

Taking the time to grieve all the big losses and small booboos that are created as we go through our often difficult and challenging lives is an essential, not optional, condition of living well.

Challenge

How do you feel about death, about your own future death and the death of those you love? How can you take steps to normalize death for yourself and those you are close to?

It might be helpful to look at how your parents raised you to think about death: was it seen as a normal, if unwanted, occurrence, or was it to be dreaded and feared at all costs? Re-examine if these transmitted beliefs actually make sense to you now.

What is your own paradigm of death and beyond? Encourage yourself to think about it and even read some books on the subject. Try to formulate your own answer to the question: What do I think will happen to me after I die? And does my answer to that question affect how I live and think about my future?

Chapter 10

Beliefs

Updating our software to reflect our current reality...

If you believe you can, or if you believe you can't, YOU'RE RIGHT!
Henry Ford

In the last eight chapters we explored the major thinking traps that can undermine our success, happiness and feelings of belonging in the world. You've also read about how I work with patients to explore their subconscious beliefs, and then help them change those beliefs for the better.

Now let's take a closer look at how you can use these same approaches to identify beliefs that may be undermining your life, keeping you stuck and unhappy – and how you can change them.

Old, Negative Beliefs Undermine Our Success

How often have you heard an adult say something like, "Oh, I'm horrible at math." "Really? How do you know? When's the last time you actually did any math?" "Well... not since I was in school, 30 years ago."

Isn't it possible that the brain has matured and developed, and that math might be easier now? Of course! But as long as we have a belief that we're not good at math, we create a future that is guided by that belief, even if it's no longer true. If a job were posted at our workplace that requires some math, we would shy away from applying for it, even if it sounds like a great job and we feel ready for a change. That's an example of a limiting belief in action.

Similarly, if I have the belief, "I am unlucky, nothing ever goes my way," when I go through a challenging event, I will cope with it according to what I believe about myself. Seeing every unfortunate event as evidence of my bad luck, I will continue in my pessimistic views, and every time something difficult happens, I'll use that as evidence that I'm simply prone to bad luck.

But if I were to believe, instead, that everyone experiences problems and hurdles in life, and if I am present and committed to resolving whatever problems life throws at me, I will see these problems as normal life challenges and seek to create the best solutions possible. Each time I overcome difficulties with my new attitude, my self-confidence grows and I come to regard myself as capable and successful, rather than unlucky.

That difference in interpretation will more than likely create a future that looks very different from the one I would create if I felt like an unlucky failure – and would be beneficial not only to my sense of well-being and happiness, but, as we've seen, to my physical health as well.

Identifying Subconscious Beliefs

It's clear that if we can replace old, negative beliefs with new, more accurate ones, we get the benefits of improved mental and physical health, better relationships, and a life of greater ease, contentment, and success (in whatever way we measure it). But how?

The first step is identifying the beliefs that are hindering us. How do we do this if the subconscious mind is hidden, by definition, and holds information we are not consciously aware of? How can we access them?

Muscle Testing

I use a technique called Applied Kinesiology (AK), or muscle testing, to better understand the subconscious mind. Muscle testing was invented by George Goodheart in 1964 for use in chiropractic work, but it is now used in other disciplines as well.

Muscle testing works on the same premise as a lie detector test. If I were to take a lie detector test, I would be hooked up to electrodes which would read slight changes in my physiology: perspiration, muscle tension, breathing, pulse, etc. Before the actual test, the questioner would ask me a few simple questions to establish my baseline norms to ensure accuracy of the results.

Then I would be asked a series of questions. When I tell the truth, I have no stress in doing so, and the electrodes don't pick up any physiological changes. However, if I lie, my body reveals the stress associated with lying with an almost imperceptible increase in sweat, tension, breathing, and other physiological responses that can be detected by the sensitive electrodes. Because it's the subconscious mind that controls our motor functions (such as muscle tension) as well as the autonomic nervous system (involuntary functions such as breathing and heartbeat), a lie detector test can detect when your body is under stress versus the baseline, revealing that your answer to a particular question is not fully truthful.

In a similar vein, muscle testing allows us to read this same stress response from "lying." Both a lie detector test and muscle testing read physiological responses that are not consciously controlled, and can pick up information revealing when the body is under stress, making muscle testing an easy and effective way to communicate with the subconscious, and better understand underlying beliefs.

I use this tool daily with patients to help us discover where they have hidden beliefs that may be at the root of their unhappiness. Using gentle pressure, we test whether a muscle is strong and locks firmly when challenged – or has a weak response – giving us powerful feedback about that person's beliefs. When something untrue is stated, the brain senses the conflict, resulting in stress, and the electrical signal from the brain to the muscle becomes restricted, resulting in a weakened muscle response. If I tell the truth, though, my muscle will stay strong when challenged.

Muscle Testing in Practice

Standing and facing my patient, I begin by first establishing their baseline strength. I ask them to hold their arm out to the side and then request that they say a truthful statement (such as their name). I gently apply downward pressure to their outstretched arm to test if they believe this statement. When they state their name, for example, there is no stress as the statement is true, and when I apply downward pressure to their arm they have no trouble resisting me and keeping their arm straight out. This is known as a "strong muscle response."

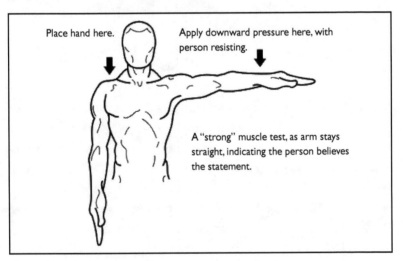

Place hand here.

Apply downward pressure here, with person resisting.

A "strong" muscle test, as arm stays straight, indicating the person believes the statement.

I then instruct my patient to say an untrue statement (by stating that their name is a false name) and again I apply gentle downward pressure to their outstretched arm. Due to the subtle stress created by stating this untruth, their arm will be weaker and I can easily press it downward with the same amount of pressure. This is known as a "weak muscle response."

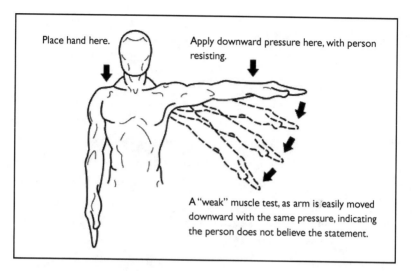

Place hand here.

Apply downward pressure here, with person resisting.

A "weak" muscle test, as arm is easily moved downward with the same pressure, indicating the person does not believe the statement.

So, if I ask my patient Tara to state, "My name is Fred," her mild internal stress reaction to this phrase causes her arm muscle to be weaker against my gentle pressure.

Each time I demonstrate this method of testing to a patient, there is always the same shocked look on their faces! They were resisting me just as hard, how come their arm was moved down so easily when they were saying a false statement? After a few more similar tests to establish their baseline, they see that the muscle testing is reliable: when they tell the truth, their arm stays strong and able to resist my pressure, when they say something untrue, the muscle is weaker, even though they are trying to resist my pressure with equal strength. Try it!

Testing Core Beliefs

Once we trust muscle testing as a tool, we can use it to test various statements and find out what we believe, subconsciously, to be true. When I initially begin to work with a patient, I like to test the following basic, core beliefs: I love myself, I have infinite worth and value, I am safe, I trust myself, I believe in myself, I set boundaries easily, I have a right to exist, and sometimes others. I'm sure you can appreciate that if we don't deep down believe these fundamental statements, this is likely the root of much of our suffering.

Once we identify any negative responses to the beliefs from the above list, we then move on to discover what other beliefs might be lurking behind the scenes that are specifically related to the particular problem my patient is having trouble with at the moment. For example, if someone is struggling with an inability to achieve their weight loss goals, we would first want to make sure they love themselves at a deep subconscious level and know their worth and value, etc. After that, we would test their beliefs around more specific phrases, such as: I eat wisely and mindfully, I use food primarily to satisfy my nutritional needs, I easily know when I am full and simply stop eating, I make good food choices for my health and well-being, and other statements designed to pinpoint underlying beliefs that are specifically getting in the way of losing weight.

While it's a bit easier to muscle test with someone else, as I do with my patients, it is possible to muscle test oneself. In Appendix A, I describe three different variations of self-testing. Try each one and see which feels most reliable to you!

Changing Limiting Beliefs

Once we have identified some of our limiting beliefs, the second step in Emotional Repatterning is changing them to more empowering beliefs.

Replacing long-held, senseless beliefs such as "I'm a failure," "I'm unlovable," "I'm a bad mother," "I'm stupid," "The world is a difficult place," "I will die of cancer because both my parents did," "My brother is better and smarter than me," with positive ones, result in profound changes in our real-world experience. When we rewire old beliefs, we open up new pathways, allowing us to create our future more intentionally.

Some of the techniques I use are easy to learn and can be practiced at home. Others require a trained facilitator to guide you. (See Resource section.) Whichever way we choose to approach it, know that while improving the conscious way we think about our lives is essential, *we gain the biggest and most impactful results by changing our subconscious mind!*

My patients are often initially skeptical that the destructive beliefs they may have held about themselves for years can be quickly transformed into beliefs that are more positive. But, it's true! Beliefs can be changed with the snap of a finger. If I suddenly come upon new information or a different perspective on something, any belief I hold can be rapidly changed. If I believe something and then am made aware of a different view or a new set of facts, my beliefs can change immediately, whether they be conscious or subconscious.

We all know that our consciously held beliefs can easily be changed. For example: if I think my husband is a faithful person and then I see him in a restaurant holding another woman's hand, I no longer believe that he is faithful. If I believe that kale is good for my health but every time I eat it I have diarrhea, that belief changes as well.

Similarly, beliefs that reside beneath our consciousness, in our subconscious, can also be easily changed. But we do so, not by having an ah-ha moment in our conscious awareness, but by using tools that "rewire" the brain around a new subconscious belief.

Changing Your Beliefs

Now I'll help you explore some of your own underlying beliefs that may be causing unhappiness, self-sabotaging behaviors, or a sense of being stuck. What are some beliefs which you suspect you may have about yourself that limit you? Thinking about these core beliefs:

*I love myself
*I am lovable
*I am safe

*I have a right to exist

*I have infinite worth and value

*I deserve the best that life has to offer

*I believe in myself

*I trust myself

*My body has all it needs to... (heal, become pregnant, defeat this cancer, etc.)

Do any of these statements make you wince a bit inside? Do any of them bring up painful memories? If so, perhaps this is a good place to begin.

Write down the beliefs from the above list that seem to stand out, and create any additional belief statements that seem more relevant to your personal situation. Notice all the statements are about "I." That's a good place to start. Also, notice that the statements are short and positively worded.

Then, using one of the self-muscle testing techniques detailed in Appendix A, test yourself to confirm which subconscious beliefs you have that are likely contributing to your problems. Because the statements are written in the positive, ideally, you would test strong to each statement, meaning you believe it. Thus, the statements that test weak are the ones we are concerned about changing.

This is one giant step forward: by bringing what is subconscious into the conscious mind, we now have a chance to work with it and change it.

"Cross-Brain" Techniques

The most effective way to replace undesirable beliefs with better ones is to employ Cross-Brain techniques. These techniques engage both the right and left sides of the brain in unison to change subconscious beliefs. I first became exposed to this idea of synching up the right and left sides of the brain about 20 years ago though a technique called Brain Gym®.

Brain Gym® was created by Paul and Gail Dennison in the

1980s. It is a series of movements designed to "wake-up" and stimulate brain function to improve focus. Using this as a starting point, I built upon the idea of using movement to improve the brain's receptivity to learning something new, in our case, a new belief.

I will teach you a simple Cross-Brain technique that is easy to use at home. It has two steps: the first step I call the Integrated Brain State, and it is followed by the Alternate Knee Tap.

Integrated Brain State – For this step we sit quietly in a chair, one ankle crossed over the other ankle, one wrist crossed over the other wrist and placing your palms together, intertwine your fingers and rest them in your lap. Repeat the new belief you desire to have (make sure to word this positively), with your eyes closed, silently, over and over again for a minute or two. When it feels complete, in that the statement now feels true to you, open your eyes.

Alternate Knee Tap – I then use this technique to "lock in" the change: standing up, start to march, lifting your knees up high. Once you have your rhythm established, keep it going and begin to tap the outside of one knee with your opposite palm, and then the other – alternating your right hand to your left knee and then your left hand to your right knee. Do this about twenty times.

These two steps rewire your brain and then lock in the new belief. It's simple but it works! How do we know? Redo your muscle test on the original statement that you were weak on. It should now test positive. (For example, if previously "I love myself" was weak during the muscle test, and this is the statement you transformed with the Cross-Brain technique, it should now result in a strong muscle test upon re-testing.)

Now take a minute and write a short to-do list that will help you incorporate the changes you've made in your subconscious into your day to day life. What can you now do differently, how can you approach situations and people differently, that would reflect the subconscious beliefs you just changed?

On Sick Leave with a Burn Out

The following case illustrates all of the practical aspects of this technique, to clarify further.

A few months ago, I began working with a patient named Karla, who was in her forties. She was off from work with a burn out. She related to me that she had had a difficult childhood as an only child of an alcoholic mother, and a father who traveled most of the time. Recent stress at work had triggered some of her traumatic memories and she became too exhausted to get out of bed in the morning. She had been in and out of therapy over the years, but the memories of her childhood still haunted her.

I spoke with her about Emotional Repatterning. We started by working with her conscious mind – using the understanding and insights Karla already had about her problems. We reviewed the numerous events that had occurred growing up as an only child, alone with her mom, events which Karla still found immensely troubling. We looked at some thinking traps that might be keeping her stuck, for example, the continuous *stories* she told herself about her childhood: that she was the victim of neglect and abuse by an alcoholic mother and an absent father. That her childhood trauma had handicapped her as an adult. That as she couldn't erase her past, she would continue to be defined by it, as she hadn't been able to move past it.

I challenged her to tell herself her story in a new way: she had survived a difficult childhood, and raised herself to become an extraordinary woman. She was in a loving marriage raising two fabulous daughters. While her childhood had been unpleasant and even traumatic at times, she had overcome so much and created a very satisfying life for herself, including a good relationship with her dad and even a functional relationship with her mom, who was still drinking. She was a true hero.

Once Karla saw that she could interpret the same facts from

a more accepting and even heroic viewpoint, she relaxed a little. It's true, she was tired of the labels: adult child of an alcoholic parent, traumatic upbringing, etc. They kept her feeling negatively tied to the past. If she could rewrite the story, seeing herself as having emerged victorious, that would be a refreshing perspective. But, of course, I knew this wouldn't be enough to really set Karla free.

As a next step, we sought to understand what subconscious beliefs Karla might have stored away as a result of all she had lived through. We used muscle testing to uncover the beliefs that were causing her to still be so vulnerable to all those memories – and to find out exactly what was being triggered.

We muscle tested a dozen or so core belief statements. She tested strong to "I love myself" (meaning she believed that statement), and strong again to "I am safe." I was pleased to see this as often a neglectful or traumatic childhood leads to a lack of self-love and a lack of feeling safe in the world. (This may be the result of actually being unsafe at times, in Karla's case in the care of a drunken parent. Though it happened more than 25 years earlier, a belief of being unsafe might very well have been underlying some of her trauma. But that was not the case.)

Then we tested the phrase, "I am lovable." As soon as Karla tested weak to this (meaning she did not believe it) she started crying. I knew we had hit a nerve. She recognized at once that it was true, that she was always working hard to convince those closest to her that she was deserving of their love. It didn't take too much to understand where this belief had come from – likely Karla had concluded as a child that because her mom chose to drink over being a present parent for her, it must have been because *she was undeserving* of her mom's love and attention – not good enough, not lovable enough, to merit it. Young children have a very hard time seeing dysfunction as the parent's fault – to a child, a parent is larger than life, so difficulties are often interpreted as their own fault.

Rather than examine why Karla concluded she was unlovable, or dredge up the specific incidents that made her believe this about herself, we simply moved on to our goal: to change Karla's belief to "I am lovable."

Believing that she is unlovable no doubt gets in the way of her emotional health and well-being. It makes no sense for her to believe this; logically and rationally she knows she is a good person, a kind person, and therefore inherently deserving of love. But her old, stuck belief blocks her from receiving, clouding her whole reality, like a pair of lenses that she doesn't even know she has on.

Using the Cross-Brain technique, we rewired that belief in Karla's subconscious to "I am lovable." Then we retested the belief to be sure it had changed: Karla repeated, "I am lovable," and I muscle tested her once again to see if her muscle was testing strong or weak to the statement. She tested strong, meaning she now believes that the statement is true – we have rewired her subconscious mind around the new belief!

This shift has the potential to create profound changes, making it much easier for Karla to move forward with new habits, actions and goals that she determines with her conscious mind – but the difference now is that she can be successful at manifesting her conscious plans because the previous obstacle, her subconscious belief, is now changed.

Our final step was writing a to-do list. We discussed, now that you both know *and believe* that you are lovable, how will your life look different? What things might you do differently? How would you expect others might relate to you now that you have this new belief? This puts into motion concrete changes that will help the new belief manifest itself clearly in her life.

In Karla's story, it can be easily understood how growing up in that environment might have led her to believe negative things about herself. But what if I had a relatively good childhood – where would subconscious beliefs like that have come from? We may never know. Very often we have no conscious memory of what might have led us to these types of beliefs. In any case, my view is, it doesn't matter: *the past is gone*. The belief is there and it limits us – that's what we do know, and that's our starting point.

Chapter 11

Conclusion

With gratitude and hopefulness....

Being alive at this time is fraught with challenges. Even though, for the majority of us, we are not consumed with the type of challenges faced by ancient cave dwellers who worried where their next meal was coming from, nor the challenges of people in the Middle Ages who worried whether they would be struck down by the Plague (experts estimate that the average lifespan then was around 31 years), life has a different set of challenges now.

For most of us reading this book, our basic, physical survival needs are being met, but our struggles are more along emotional lines: how to live well, how to find peace (if not happiness), how to navigate relationships more skillfully, how to find satisfaction, well-being and purpose in our lives. Against the backdrop of a planet which is in an increasingly precarious state, somehow the urgency for us to "get it right" feels even greater.

It takes an enormous amount of humility to look deeply at ourselves, and consider that we might have a larger-than-imagined role to play in our own unhappiness: not external circumstances, not our boss, nor our spouse, nor our neighbor. Taking personal responsibility is essential, as it is the beginning of our empowerment to greatly change the quality of our experience in our lives.

Many people think that taking responsibility for their role in certain dynamics means admitting that they were wrong. "So what?" I say! If we accept that we are here to learn and evolve, of course there are incidences – many, many incidences – of us being "wrong." There is no shame in that. No one is perfect; I'm quite sure if they were perfect they wouldn't be here, they'd be frolicking around in the afterlife somewhere, eating red velvet cupcakes and not gaining any weight.

Wouldn't it be nice if we had enough kindness toward ourselves to look back on our failings and not see ourselves as a failure?

Rather than blame ourselves, can we find gratitude? Gratitude for the opportunity to see ourselves clearly and to learn and grow from our new understanding? Followed up with a big dose of hopefulness? Hopefulness that the pieces that are still hard for us will become easier. When hope is absent, bitterness, cynicism and sarcasm take its place. Can we stay in a place of gratitude for what is, hopeful for what may still be?

The Eight Spheres of Emotion

In this book, I have looked at eight spheres where emotions and thoughts easily get tangled up and cause an enormous amount of suffering and unhappiness.

Without *Self-love* and deep *Acceptance* of how things are, it is difficult to move forward, particularly when life sends us challenges. Without taking *Responsibility* for the *Stories* we make up in our heads about how things are, and owning our role in every relationship and situation we are a part of, we bypass opportunities to learn and author a better future for ourselves. Without understanding that our lives are a *Co-Creation* and acknowledging that we are loved, supported and helped – via nudges and well-timed, hand-selected *Gifts* – by the Universe to achieve what we have come here to accomplish, the way forward can feel very lonely and difficult. *Regrets* and fears of the unknown, *Death* being at the top of the list, can easily paralyze us from moving forward. To be human is to suffer, for the majority of us, and suffering often results in wisdom. We are here to become wise, so why resist?

Given this paradigm, can we bring suffering to a minimum

and wisdom to a maximum in a shorter timeframe? Yes, I believe we can and see evidence of it daily in my work with patients. Identifying and changing limiting beliefs helps us get out of our own way. Whether you learn these techniques yourself or find a practitioner to work with, the rapid change that comes about from rewiring your brain's subconscious programming can produce quick and painless shifts in perception.

My goal in writing this book is to share the common threads in our human experience of living that need to be better understood and more skillfully maneuvered and healed, to allow us to move forward with less suffering and greater ease.

My insights come from being broken open through my family's struggle during Ben's illness, and through years of working with patients, who have been the greatest of teachers.

My true hope is that each reader can recognize themselves in the stories which were shared throughout this book and, from the wisdom accumulated, move forward to a more fulfilling life, lived with fewer limits and greater emotional ease.

Be the Change You Wish to See in the World.
Gandhi

From the Author

Thank you for purchasing *Emotional Repatterning: Healing Emotional Pain by Rewiring the Brain.* My true hope is that you derived as much from reading the book as I have in writing it. If you have a few moments, please feel free to add your review of the book to your favorite online site for feedback.

Also, if you would like to connect with other books that I have coming in the near future, please visit my website for news on upcoming works, recent blog posts or to sign up for my monthly newsletter: https://www.lisasamet.com

Sincerely, Lisa Samet, N.D.

Appendix A

Self-Muscle Testing Options

1. Sway Method:
First, I define for myself that if the statement is true I will sway forward and if the statement is false, I will sway backward. Then, standing with my feet slightly apart, chin level and eyes looking down, I say aloud a statement I know to be true – my name is Lisa. I wait and see that I sway forward. Then I tell a lie – my name is Henry – and wait to see that I sway backward. If so, I am well-calibrated for my session and ready to test my subconscious beliefs.

2. Finger Pull:
Sitting comfortably, I make a circle with my thumb and ring finger. With my other hand, I place the fingertips of my thumb and index finger together. I then insert this *part way* into my finger circle. I then say a truth – my name is Lisa – and separate my thumb-index fingers, trying to pull apart the circle. At the same time, I try to resist and keep the circle closed. If I say a truth, something I believe, the circle will stay strong and closed against my effort. If the phrase, however, is untrue, not something I believe, I will easily be able to open the circle as it will be weak against my effort to pull it apart.

3. Pointer as Shoulder:
I place my open hand, palm down on my sternum, right below my neck. With that same hand, I raise my index finger up off my chest an inch or so. I say a true statement, and then with the index finger of my other hand, gently try to press down on my raised index finger. If the phrase is true, my raised finger should stay strong and elevated against my pressure. If the phrase is

false, the raised index will weaken and be easily pushed down to my chest with my other finger.

References

1. Ed Diener and Micaela Chan, "Happy People Live Longer: Subjective Well-Being Contributes to Health and Longevity," *Applied Psychology: Health and Well-Being* 3, no.1 (March 2011): 1–44.
2. Ibid.
3. Michael Lemonick, "The Biology of Joy," Time, January 9, 2005.
4. Yoichi Chida & Andrew Steptoe, "Positive Psychological Well-being and Mortality: A Quantitative Review of Perspective Observational Studies," *Psychosomatic Medicine* 70, no. 7 (Sept 2008): 740–58.
5. Erik J. Giltay et al., "Dispositional Optimism and All-Cause and Cardiovascular Mortality in a Prospective Cohort of Elderly Dutch Men and Women," *Archives of General Psychiatry* 61, no.11 (Nov 2004): 1125–38.
6. Christopher Peterson and Mechele E. De Avila, "Optimistic Explanatory Style andthe Perception of Health Problems," *Journal of Clinical Psychology* 51, no.1 (January 1995): 128–35; Katri Raikkonen et al., "Effects of Optimism, Pessimism, and Trait Anxiety on Ambulatory Blood Pressure and Mood During Everyday Life," *Journal of Personality and Social Psychology* 76, no.1 (Jan 1999): 104–14; Kymberley K. Bennett and Marta Elliott, "Pessimistic Explanatory Style and Cardiac Health: What is the Relation and the Mechanism that Links Them?" *Basic and Applied Social Psychology* 27, no.3 (Sept 2005): 238–48.

Resources & Recommended Reading

Belief Change and Energy Psychology Modalities

Psych-K: Highly recommended. Info on training or how to find a practitioner: *psych-k.com*

Emotional Freedom Technique (EFT): AAMET International is a unique, not-for-profit global association of dedicated EFT (Emotional Freedom Techniques) practitioners, trainers and students. *aametinternational.org*

Theta Healing: a meditation training technique utilizing a spiritual philosophy for improvement and evolvement of mind, body and spirit. *thetahealing.com*

Recommended Reading

Loving What Is (Katie), *How to Change Your Mind* (Pollan),), *The Untethered Soul* (Singer), *The Four Agreements* (Ruiz), *Broken Open* (Lesser), *Daring Greatly* (Brown), *Pussy* (Thomashauer), *The Wisdom of the Enneagram* (Riso), *The Universe Has Your Back* (Bernstein), *The Conscious Parent* (Tsabary), *The Emotion Code* (Nelson), *Biology of Belief* (Lipton), *Dying to Be Me* (Moorjani), *A Neurosurgeon's Journey Through the Afterlife* (Alexander, documentary).

O-BOOKS

SPIRITUALITY

O is a symbol of the world, of oneness and unity; this eye represents knowledge and insight. We publish titles on general spirituality and living a spiritual life. We aim to inform and help you on your own journey in this life.
If you have enjoyed this book, why not tell other readers by posting a review on your preferred book site?

Recent bestsellers from O-Books are:

Heart of Tantric Sex
Diana Richardson
Revealing Eastern secrets of deep love and intimacy to Western couples.
Paperback: 978-1-90381-637-0 ebook: 978-1-84694-637-0

Crystal Prescriptions
The A-Z guide to over 1,200 symptoms and their healing crystals
Judy Hall
The first in the popular series of six books, this handy little guide is packed as tight as a pill-bottle with crystal remedies for ailments.
Paperback: 978-1-90504-740-6 ebook: 978-1-84694-629-5

Take Me To Truth
Undoing the Ego
Nouk Sanchez, Tomas Vieira
The best-selling step-by-step book on shedding the Ego, using the
teachings of *A Course In Miracles*.
Paperback: 978-1-84694-050-7 ebook: 978-1-84694-654-7

The 7 Myths about Love...Actually!
The Journey from your HEAD to the HEART of your SOUL
Mike George
Smashes all the myths about LOVE.
Paperback: 978-1-84694-288-4 ebook: 978-1-84694-682-0

The Holy Spirit's Interpretation of the New Testament
A Course in Understanding and Acceptance
Regina Dawn Akers
Following on from the strength of *A Course In Miracles*, NTI
teaches us how to experience the love and oneness of God.
Paperback: 978-1-84694-085-9 ebook: 978-1-78099-083-5

The Message of A Course In Miracles
A translation of the Text in plain language
Elizabeth A. Cronkhite
A translation of *A Course in Miracles* into plain, everyday
language for anyone seeking inner peace. The companion
volume, *Practicing A Course In Miracles*, offers practical lessons
and mentoring.
Paperback: 978-1-84694-319-5 ebook: 978-1-84694-642-4

Thinker's Guide to God
Peter Vardy
An introduction to key issues in the philosophy of religion.
Paperback: 978-1-90381-622-6

Your Simple Path
Find Happiness in every step
Ian Tucker
A guide to helping us reconnect with what is really important in our lives.
Paperback: 978-1-78279-349-6 ebook: 978-1-78279-348-9

365 Days of Wisdom
Daily Messages To Inspire You Through The Year
Dadi Janki
Daily messages which cool the mind, warm the heart and guide you along your journey.
Paperback: 978-1-84694-863-3 ebook: 978-1-84694-864-0

Body of Wisdom
Women's Spiritual Power and How it Serves
Hilary Hart
Bringing together the dreams and experiences of women across the world with today's most visionary spiritual teachers.
Paperback: 978-1-78099-696-7 ebook: 978-1-78099-695-0

Dying to Be Free
From Enforced Secrecy to Near Death to True Transformation
Hannah Robinson
After an unexpected accident and near-death experience, Hannah Robinson found herself radically transforming her life, while a remarkable new insight altered her relationship with her father, a practising Catholic priest.
Paperback: 978-1-78535-254-6 ebook: 978-1-78535-255-3

The Ecology of the Soul
A Manual of Peace, Power and Personal Growth for Real People
in the Real World
Aidan Walker
Balance your own inner Ecology of the Soul to regain your
natural state of peace, power and wellbeing.
Paperback: 978-1-78279-850-7 ebook: 978-1-78279-849-1

Not I, Not other than I
The Life and Teachings of Russel Williams
Steve Taylor, Russel Williams
The miraculous life and inspiring teachings of one of the World's
greatest living Sages.
Paperback: 978-1-78279-729-6 ebook: 978-1-78279-728-9

On the Other Side of Love
A woman's unconventional journey towards wisdom
Muriel Maufroy
When life has lost all meaning, what do you do?
Paperback: 978-1-78535-281-2 ebook: 978-1-78535-282-9

Practicing A Course In Miracles
A translation of the Workbook in plain language, with
mentor's notes
Elizabeth A. Cronkhite
The practical second and third volumes of The Plain-Language
A Course In Miracles.
Paperback: 978-1-84694-403-1 ebook: 978-1-78099-072-9

Quantum Bliss
The Quantum Mechanics of Happiness, Abundance, and Health
George S. Mentz
Quantum Bliss is the breakthrough summary of success and spirituality secrets that customers have been waiting for.
Paperback: 978-1-78535-203-4 ebook: 978-1-78535-204-1

The Upside Down Mountain
Mags MacKean
A must-read for anyone weary of chasing success and happiness – one woman's inspirational journey swapping the uphill slog for the downhill slope.
Paperback: 978-1-78535-171-6 ebook: 978-1-78535-172-3

Your Personal Tuning Fork
The Endocrine System
Deborah Bates
Discover your body's health secret, the endocrine system, and 'twang' your way to sustainable health!
Paperback: 978-1-84694-503-8 ebook: 978-1-78099-697-4

Readers of ebooks can buy or view any of these bestsellers by clicking on the live link in the title. Most titles are published in paperback and as an ebook. Paperbacks are available in traditional bookshops. Both print and ebook formats are available online.
Find more titles and sign up to our readers' newsletter at http://www.johnhuntpublishing.com/mind-body-spirit
Follow us on Facebook at https://www.facebook.com/OBooks/
and Twitter at https://twitter.com/obooks